ONCE A FAN

ONCE A FAN

WHY IT IS SO HARD TO BE A SPORTS FAN

JIM CHERNESKY

iUniverse, Inc.
Bloomington

Once a Fan
Why It Is So Hard to Be a Sports Fan

iUniverse books may be ordered through booksellers or by contacting:

iUniverse
1663 Liberty Drive
Bloomington, IN 47403
www.iuniverse.com
1-800-Authors (1-800-288-4677)

ISBN: 978-1-4759-5489-0 (sc)
ISBN: 978-1-4759-5490-6 (ebk)

Library of Congress Control Number: 2012919117

Printed in the United States of America

iUniverse rev. date:11/05/2012

To all sports fans in all sports, in all countries, be they amateur or professional, male or female, black or white. To those of you who share the passion and excitement of watching and competing in your sport, I tip my hat to all of you and to those who, like me, were *Once a Fan*.

To my wife and three boys, daughter-in-law and granddaughter, parents, sisters, extended family, and friends who supported and reinforced the principles that I held dear throughout this experience.

Finally, to the players, teams, teammates, and friends who shared this journey. Your names have been changed but the bond is there. It has been an honor to share the field with you.

I never meant for this book to be a study in accuracy; it is not a product of years of historical research. It is somewhere between 100 percent accurate and a fisherman's exaggeration of the one that got away. In some cases, I embellished and added some drama, but only to enhance the memory and make a point. That's okay, though, because it's my book!

CONTENTS

PREFACE

Once upon a time, not too long ago, there was a boy who lived in a good and wholesome place with the sports he loved and the men who made it great. His passion was to watch his heroes play the game, to emulate them on and off the field, to hang their pictures on his bedroom wall. He revered them not only because they were outstanding competitors and performers in their respective sports, but also because they exuded a passion and a respect for the game that was undeniable.

These heroes grew up in the Depression and through World War II. They played their respective sports with an intensity to win but with the grace and sportsmanship to accept defeat and acknowledge the efforts of the winner.

As the boy grew older, he began to see glimpses of the backroom of the sports and the darker underlayer of the heroes that he idolized. He watched in growing disappointment as collegiate and professional sports and the athletes who played the game were gradually swallowed up by greed and big business. League expansions, trade deadlines, arbitration, salary caps, and, oh yes, the press had diluted and cheapened the sports and his heroes to the point where it was not only financially impossible to attend the games in person, but also just not fun to watch anymore. Teams changed rosters every year. Steadfast hometown heroes in all sports left town for bigger paychecks and commercial deals.

Jim Chernesky

There are many sports-minded young fans out there who accept the present conditions because that's all they have known. There are some boys out there, like the one in this book, who remember the way it was, don't like the way it is now, and wish that it could be the way it was again.

CHAPTER 1

The Golden Years: 1954 to 1964

You can always look at any time in history and apply this quote from Charles Dickens: "It was the best of times, and it was the worst of times." I talked to my parents about their childhood and got the feeling of what it might have been like to grow up with Prohibition and the poverty of the 1920s, coming on the heels of World War I. The 1930s brought on the Great Depression, and by the time families and children made it through that, it was time for World War II, which lasted from 1938 to 1945. Just when it looked as though there was a light at the end of the tunnel for this generation, we saw the Korean War as a bruise on our backside. By the mid-1950s, however, there was a ten-year period from 1954 to 1964, which seemed to signal that the last of the storm clouds had passed and the sun was shining.

This journey begins in Bridgeport, Connecticut, an average industrial city during the 1950s. It was a time of postwar pride and American values. The population was exploding. Soldiers were returning from the war with an opportunity to reunite with families and get on with a normal life. There was optimism and spirit in the air, and baseball was America's national pastime.

Growing Up on Hooker Road

My earliest recollection of this wonderful time was the summer of 1954. It was an especially hot summer, and I spent much of my time outdoors in the front yard. We had a great old maple tree in front of our house, and we would spread out a blanket and take toys and snacks and hang out under the tree. Even on the hottest days, the tree seemed to wrap its arms around us; it defined the limits of my world in that front yard. My sister Laurie was barely two years old, and my sister Cindy was four years away from making her grand entrance. My grandfather had come up from Wilkes-Barre, Pennsylvania, that summer and tried to keep me occupied while Grandma helped Mom and Dad with Laurie.

We didn't have a swimming pool and didn't go to the beach, but we seemed to have everything we needed in that front patch of lawn on Hooker Road. My grandfather would peel oranges and sit in his old metal rocker in a tank top T-shirt and make sure I didn't run out into the street. We both had tans that year that Panama Jack would have been proud of.

It's funny, at the tender age of four, how small your perception of the world can be. I did not travel beyond the four corners of the yard. I did not visit neighbors. Even though I could stand in our driveway and see the sloping roof and the red brick façade of Thomas Hooker School one block over, it might as well have been in Kentucky for all I knew.

The other remarkable thing about our neighborhood was the lack of street traffic. Oh, there was an occasional car that went by our house, but for the most part it was very quiet. We had a milkman who actually delivered bottle of milk to our doorstep. He worked for one of the local dairies. You also had a choice of eggs and even ice cream delivered, and you could indicate your order on a checklist that he would leave at the door. Eventually the dairies provided an aluminum box with a lid that was somewhat insulated. You could put a few quart bottles of milk in the box along with a dozen eggs or other small items, and it would keep for a while without the summer sun spoiling it.

Our mailman walked! Yes, he walked from house to house. He had no truck, car, bike, or scooter. He was dressed in blue and always carried a large leather bag with a protective flap. Even at five years old, I often wondered how he got to our house. He would just appear, walking down the street. There was no car, no bus, he didn't just drop out of the sky, and I was sure his mother didn't drive him.

To round out this interesting group, we had two very unique additions to the cast. The first was someone we referred to as the "Rag Man." The Rag Man was an old grizzly man dressed in clothes he obviously found in a box of old paint rags. He sat on top of an old horse-drawn wagon with huge wooden wheels that looked like they could fall off at any minute. This entire flea market on wheels was filled with old clothes and other items that looked as though they had seen better days. The old horse seemed to be as far along in life as the driver sitting on top of the wagon. I was never really sure about the purpose of the Rag Man. I never saw anyone put anything in the wagon. I never saw anyone try to take something off the wagon, and no money was ever exchanged. As a matter of fact, the only time I ever saw the wagon really come to a halt was when the horse decided to drop one of his conspicuous loads in the middle of the street. After a few minutes of the pause that refreshes, horse and rider would continue along their way. You could hear the squeaks and groans of the wagon and the steady clop, clop, clop of the horse's hooves on the hot black pavement. The old man stared straight ahead and never talked to anyone except for an occasional call of "Raaaags!"

These little fragments of memorabilia paint a picture of a small, safe world that was always under a watchful eye from the kitchen window. This feeling of safety was one that I always wanted to pass on as a father if given the chance. Gradually, as I grew more familiar with this safe haven, my world started to expand, and foreign elements began to challenge my safe playground.

Off to School

My small and protected world began to grow in the fall of 1955, with my first day of school. Miss Seller's kindergarten class might as well have been a two-hour commute to New York City to a job on Wall Street. In those days, going to school could be traumatic for some five-year-olds. In many homes, fathers worked and mothers stayed home and cooked, cleaned, and watched the children. There was no day care, no preschool or nursery school. There was no reason to drop a one-year-old off at the sitter's. At five years old, you were pushed out of the nest and into the fray for the first time.

There were many tears and cleanly dressed classmates clinging to the legs of their mothers that first day. Gradually, Miss Seller worked the class into a routine of songs, artwork, lunch, and recess that made the morning session go by a little smoother.

My first official documented act in the sports world was making my own baseball cap in kindergarten. To this day, my parents remember me walking down the street toward our house with that baseball cap. It was my first uniform.

The interesting thing about my class was that the group of students remained 95 percent intact by the time we all advanced to eighth grade in the same building. It was the same school, same building, same group of students and friends.

I realize that many people had similar experiences in school; I don't mean to imply that mine was something special. What is relevant about these days was how small and predictable the world was. We accepted things as they were. Schedules were the same, and neighborhoods stayed the same. It wasn't just our neighborhood; this feeling of "Wonder Bread" wholesomeness permeated the national scene; it was even reflected in our music and our entertainment.

Television of the Fifties

When we weren't in school, we were either playing outdoors or watching our favorite shows on television. Television then was not taken for granted; not everyone had a set. Televisions were also exclusively black and white. There was no cable, no high-definition digital screens, and only a few channels. During the week, my favorite show was the original *Mickey Mouse Club*. Every day at five o'clock, I was allowed to bring my dinner plate into the living room and sit on the floor in front of the TV and be one of the Mouseketeers.

In those early days, bedtime was very close to eight o'clock, and with no homework in kindergarten or first grade, there was nothing keeping us from that curfew. As my sisters and I got a little older, we were able to sneak in some evening shows such as *The Honeymooners* or *Ozzie and Harriet*. It was good old all American day-to-day living on the lighter side. There were no four-letter words and no reference to sex or sleeping together every five minutes. In fact, most of these shows were so pure that any bedroom conversation by mom and dad was done in a bedroom that had double beds.

By the late '50s, however, there were rumblings under the earthly crust of television that was looking to stain the white sheets of our television mores. *The Ed Sullivan Show* introduced Elvis Presley, a young teenage rock and roller. Elvis not only belted out songs that defied any previous musical experiences of its kind, but his physical gyrations and dancing caused a stir on the networks. It was such an exception to what had been shown in the past that the network was directed to only show Elvis from the waist up while he was performing.

At least with Elvis, you knew what was coming, and as a parent you could have your children hide their eyes if you were so inclined. *The Adventures of Ozzie and Harriet* was another problem. This was yet another in a string of family-based everyday situation comedies that lulled you into a family-oriented fun and harmless half hour. Things were comfortable until the last five minutes of the show, when youngest son, teen idol Ricky, would come out and sing one of his songs to close the show. He often performed in the setting of a high school dance, where he sang with his backup band.

When I look back at those television clips now, compared to things that eight- and nine-year-olds are watching these days, I can't help but smile. Today, television's marketing strategy seems to be trying to outdo each other with more sex, more violence, and more extreme behavior. You can only stand by and shake your head.

Saturdays in the fifties not only meant a day with no school, it also meant a morning of cartoons, which were not available at any other time of the week. One of my favorites in this all-star lineup was Mighty Mouse.

Might Mouse was the rodent version of Superman, another great show of the comic book–inspired decade. Mighty Mouse would usually come to the aid of his fellow mice, especially cute female mice, when the black cat gang decided it was time to cause some trouble. To this day, over fifty years later, I can still sing along to the opening theme:

Mr. Trouble never hangs around

When he hears this mighty sound:

"Here I come to save the day!"

That means that Mighty Mouse is on the way.

Mighty Mouse was another positive symbol at the time that, even in an animated form, where good prevailed over evil, and our heroes were alive and well and protecting us. It felt great to be a kid.

Cowboys and Soldiers and Idols

Our heroes of the times were not just centered on sports and cartoons. Television was also sprinkled generously with movies and shows depicting the Old West and our armed servicemen in battle, since World War II had ended only ten short years prior. The nation was still fresh off the patriotism, pride, and nationalistic union of winning a world war on two fronts. We had emerged as the world leader, second to none. The term "Made in Japan" was synonymous with junk and poor quality. My, how times have changed!

In addition to pride in our military, we were also deeply interested in American history. Cowboy movies and shows abounded: Roy Rogers (before the hamburger restaurant), the Lone Ranger, Wild Bill Hickok, Gene Autry, Hopalong Cassidy; the list just goes on. The Old West scenarios were mixed with some cultural modernization that escaped most naïve ten-year-olds. Pat Brady, sidekick to Roy Rogers, drove a Jeep, which looked circa World War II. Where Pat got a Jeep from back in the Old West never seemed to pique anyone's curiosity. We just took it at face value and enjoyed the adventure.

Our soldiers, sailors, and Marines were also glamorized and paid tribute to in the fifties and early sixties. With John Wayne, the famous Hollywood actor of the times, led the charge, movie after movie came out depicting the great contributions of our heroes in uniform. With all of these shoot-'em-up westerns and army battles for our viewing pleasure, it was no wonder that every self-respecting American boy under the age of fourteen wanted the latest in western gear and army issue. Even into the early sixties, movies such as *Sands of Iwo Jima*, *Bataan*, and *The Longest Day* revisited some of the key battles and heroic deeds of the war. Young boys, including my friends and me, reenacted these battles in our backyards and local woods. We were all equipped with replicas of army helmets, rifles, hand grenades, and bayonets. We would assemble a group of eight to twelve young neighborhood soldiers and spend hours hunting and shooting each other. As long as we were home for dinner and did our homework, our parents had no other issues with our recreational pastime.

Television also devoted its fair share to our sports heroes at the time. New York Yankee and Brooklyn Dodger games were occasionally televised on WPIX Channel 11 and WOR TV Channel 9 during the summer. Although the games were in black and white and for the most part viewed on twelve-inch television screens, to a boy of seven or eight years old, it was just like being at the stadium.

I may be sticking my neck out here but these televised games and their promotional activities seemed to be more focused on the youth of America than they are today. *Happy Felton's Knot-Hole Gang* was a television program led by an old vaudeville comic. Happy would appear in a Dodger uniform and bring local Little Leaguers together with some of the Major League stars of the time to help these young players improve their game and have more fun in the process. The instruction always included little reminders of fair play and good sportsmanship. You would be hard pressed to find a similar show with this type of audience and emphasis today. Today after most games, sports figures undergo a verbal autopsy by the press on the reasons for their personal physical and mental lapses during the game. *The Knot-Hole Gang* focused on the positive and how to improve, while recognizing that mistakes and miscues of judgment are just as much part of the game as scoring the winning touchdown or banging out the winning hit. Incidentally, the term "Knot-Hole Gang" originated from a practice back at the turn of the century and certainly through the depression years of young boys sneaking a peak at a baseball game through the knot-holes in the wooden fences that surrounded baseball fields. With no television and no money for a ticket, it was the only way a young boy could feed his passion.

My early days of school also had a significant influence on this golden era I was experiencing; my world continued to expand outside my front yard and the one-block walk to school every day. Teachers and new classmates began to populate my world. About this time, I started to develop a close friendship with Billy Vance. Billy only lived a block away, but prior to this, I rarely went over to anyone's house that wasn't a relative. One of the culturally significant things about this budding relationship is that Billy had an older sister, Barbara. So whenever I was over there, we were constantly in the company of and influenced by an older, cooler crowd.

Although we were younger, this gave us an opportunity to dip our hands into the pool of the local teenage culture, not knowing that by 1960 it would vanish forever. Customized old cars, rock and roll music, slang talk, and slick hairstyles were all the rage. Barbara's boyfriend, Bob, had a 1959 black Chevy Impala with spinner wheel covers. He probably washed that car more than he washed himself; he was always outside during the summer in a white T-shirt and his slicked-back hair, walking around that car with a soft cloth, looking for water spots.

My early relationship with Billy was fuel to this ever-burning passion of watching and participating in sports during these wonderful years. We fed off of each other's enthusiasm for the competition, the fraternal team feeling, and just the aesthetics of playing games in this time of innocence. The fun of watching sporting events and especially participating during this golden age was that the emphasis truly was on the enjoyment of the game. Playing the game, whatever it was, with others who shared the interest for the love of it. Everyone wanted to win but it was okay to lose. We shook hands anyway. There wasn't the same emphasis on athletic excellence. You brought your best skills and you were accepted for that. There were no soccer camps, no endless drills for shooting fouls, no batting cages. You just played, got dirty, and then went home for dinner. Under these long-forgotten conditions, kids of all ages wanted to participate.

These were simple times, they were innocent times. Yes, we managed to get into trouble sometimes, and we had our share of arguments and disagreements, but it was usually over a broken window or a controversial play. No one was really hurt and no one was thrown in jail. We didn't have a lot of money but it never seemed that we needed it. We made our own fun.

Cub Scouts

Back in Mrs. Anderson's fourth grade class, I sat next to Johnny Keen. There were two things that I remember about Johnny. One is that he was a great artist for a fourth-grader. He may have motivated me to lean more toward art, drawing, and painting about this time in my life. The other and more significant observation was that every Tuesday, Johnny would wear his Cub Scout uniform to school (his meetings were Tuesday nights in the school auditorium). I thought that was really cool to have a uniform like that.

I convinced my father that I wanted to be a Cub Scout, and he tracked down the pack leader, Mr. Benson, for an application. All I knew about Cub Scouts was that they wore a neat uniform and I would probably look good in it.

Cub Scouts must have been started by a group of former soldiers who returned from service and really missed walking around in the underbrush in the rain and the mud. They must have longed to eat overcooked food from a campfire and wash themselves from water in their helmet and sleep in a smelly canvas tent, trying to keep the bugs out of their sleeping bag. Fortunately, that part of scouts was only a week or two out of the school year. Most of the time, we met at the school and built birdhouses and completed a variety of achievements and electives from our scout's manual.

Beyond the uniform and some of the activities, scouts were certainly part of the fabric and the culture of this golden era. It was a time of friendship, team unification, patriotism, and community service. People cared about other people and what they were doing. We had not yet crossed the river into the "every man for himself" attitude of today.

Cub Scouts also became the springboard for my first involvement in team sports. The Cub Scout softball league, collecting baseball cards, watching all my favorite baseball idols on television, and expanding my circle of friends all contributed to an incredibly fertile field for this budding sports enthusiast. Little did I know that these times of innocence, enthusiasm, and positive outlook would begin to erode with new events and attitudes looming on the horizon. It didn't matter, however; the die had already been cast. The golden era had opened a path for me, and there was no turning back.

The End of an Era

This ten-year span seemed to parallel the best and most memorable years of sports in my lifetime. As this golden age started to wane, so it seemed that my golden age of sports started to show cracks in its armor. One by one, as we moved into the early sixties, it seemed that the seeds of discontent started chipping away, signaling the end of the idyllic world of sports that I had come to know. The Dodgers left Brooklyn for Los Angeles, California. The Yankees then fired the beloved manager Casey Stengel after the 1960 World Series.

On the home front, the teenage crowd graduated and Bob (Billy's sister's boyfriend) sold his Impala and went off into the service. How Barbara sobbed that day at the front door. It was like a funeral. I could feel things changing, feel the shifting sands of time moving under me. I was struggling to plant my feet on some new and sturdy ground.

This eroding of the golden era seemed to level off for a while, as I was about to enjoy several years of Little League baseball.

Changes seemed to occur more rapidly at this time. The American Football League formed. In October 1963, the Los Angeles Dodgers swept the New York Yankees in the World Series. Sandy Koufax had pitched masterfully in two wins. Looking back, that Series was probably the death blow to the Yankee dynasty. The Yankees managed another World Series in 1964 but seemed to drift into the background after that for a few years. This was also the time that Mickey Mantle was moved from centerfield to first base. The sun was setting on the Yankees that I knew.

A mere one month after the Dodger sweep of the Yankees in the 1963 World Series, one solitary event seemed to bring down the curtain on what I considered to be the golden era. That event was the day in Dallas when President John F. Kennedy was assassinated. I will never forget that day; most people who were around can remember what they were doing when they herd the news. It was about one o'clock on a crisp November afternoon, a few days before Thanksgiving. I had just come in from my post as school crossing guard. I walked into my homeroom to hang up my coat and Mrs. Blake, my teacher, was sitting at her desk, crying. She sadly announced to my classmates coming in that the president had been shot and his survival was very doubtful. We spent the rest of the afternoon trying to listen to radio updates and pretend to work. When the announcement finally came on that he was dead, a shock fell over the school like nothing I had ever seen. We had learned about Abraham Lincoln and John Wilkes Booth, but we had never actually experienced anything like this firsthand.

The day of the president's funeral, classes were canceled and schools were empty and dark. I remember watching the caisson wagons on television slowly lumbering up Pennsylvania Avenue in Washington with the president's flag-draped casket. I had that feeling that the world would never be the same again. It would be almost forty year later on September 11, 2001, that I would have that same feeling again.

The spring of 1964 brought graduation and a change to a new school and new friends and priorities. I said good-bye to many friends and tried to hang on to as many as I could. I guess for me, I was trying to distinguish the difference between just growing up and moving on, and the world going to hell in a hand basket. I wasn't really sure what the future was going to look like. I wasn't sure about how to move forward. The only thing I was certain of is that there would be no going back. The golden age as I knew it . . . was gone forever.

CHAPTER 2

Attitude Adjustment

It's difficult to imagine my childhood years without a list of idols or at least prominent figures that I wanted to emulate. During my formative years, we lived in a time of prosperous baby boomers and a nation fresh off of World War II.

Everyone's list of heroes, mentors, or at least people you looked up to, should include your father. My father was that for me, and for whatever he was or wasn't, he was always there for us and really gave me my first love of sports. A die-hard Brooklyn Dodger fan himself, my father loved baseball. He also watched football, but during the 1950s, baseball was the sport of preference. I was about ten months old in October 1951 when New York Giants outfielder Bobby Thompson hit the "Shot Heard 'Round the World." His home run off of Dodger pitcher Ralph Branca won the sudden death playoff game and vaulted the Giants into their unlikely trip to the World Series. This was the final nail in the coffin after the Dodgers had squandered a thirteen-game league lead during the months of August and September.

Part of my attitude and love for sports, yes, my very values about what were important, came from sharing these types of games and bonding experiences with my family and friends. These early experiences with my parents became the pillars of what I held on to as important and the reasons why, later in life, I wanted so much to be a dad.

Somehow, as an impressionable young boy surrounded by a supportive family and these brave, strong, upright sports and television idols, I felt safe, protected, and optimistic that every day would be better than the one before.

You would guess by now that with my intense love of sports my list of boyhood idols would be heavily seasoned with athletes, especially baseball players, and you'd be right. My first exposure to baseball, at the ripe old age of four, came at the hands of my father. Before I could recite the entire alphabet, I could name the starting lineup and most of the pitchers who graced the diamond at Ebbets Field. Gil Hodges, Jim Gilliam, Pee Wee Reese, Duke Snider, Roy Campanella, Carl Furillo (or Friddo as I called him), Carl Erskine—the list goes on. Come to think of it, I could, at the ripe old age of sixty today, do the same thing for the New York Yankees of the late 1950s and early 1960s. Players such as Bill Skowron, Bobby Richardson, Tony Kubek, Clete Boyer, Roger Maris, Yogi Berra, Whitey Ford, Billy Martin, and Mickey Mantle are forever etched in my memories.

Reciting those lineups was more than just a cheap parlor trick of random memorization. I could remember those lineups at age six and again at sixty because they never changed. You could count on them staying with the team and coming back to spring training the following year. They weren't going to arbitration, looking for a new contract, or jumping to a new team late in their career just to finally play in a World Series. Fans knew their teams and loved their teams, win or lose. There were no postgame interviews with managers and players listing all the excuses why they didn't win the day's game. Ernie Banks, the great shortstop of the Chicago Cubs, played close to twenty years and never came close to being in a World Series. He never played for anyone but the Chicago Cubs, and his favorite expression was always, "Let's play two" (games).

The Mick

Mickey Mantle was undoubtedly one of the most dynamic players of his time and truly my most influential sports idol. Mickey played his first game for the Yankees in 1951, eventually replacing Joe DiMaggio in center field. During his eighteen-year career with the Yankees, the switch-hitting slugger hit 536 home runs and was voted the American League Most Valuable Player three times. Throughout his career, Mantle was plagued by injuries and leg pain, caused by osteomyelitis, yet he persevered to leave one of the greatest baseball legacies of all time. He was elected to baseball's Hall of Fame in 1974.

No single player could create such awe and excitement for me just by walking out of the dugout than the Mick. He had incredibly broad shoulders and a huge neck, and in an age before last names were common on the backs of uniforms, all you needed to see was the pinstripe uniform with the number 7 on the back and, unless you were from a Mars, you knew who it was.

Part of the reason why I looked up to him so much was not only his physical ability, it was also his attitude. He obviously loved the game. He smiled that Oklahoma farm boy smile until his later years, when the pain of his injuries made every game a mountain to climb. His love and enthusiasm for the game was infectious. Even in today's modern age of diet supplements, high-tech weight-training programs, and steroids, I have never seen anyone in baseball hit a ball harder or farther than he did.

While he was still basically a rookie player in 1955, he launched a home run off Washington Senators pitcher Chuck Stobbs that was measured at 565 feet. Later in his career at Yankee Stadium, he hit a ball that hit the top of the façade in right field, the last barrier before going completely out of the stadium. Later, math and physics buffs estimated that with its upward trajectory, if it had not hit the façade of the roof, the ball would have traveled more than 600 feet. Even ground balls that he hit were hit so hard, that your first impression as an infielder was to jump into a foxhole instead of trying to catch it.

When he did hit one of his 536 home runs, the other significant sign of his attitude toward the sport, his team, and the opposing players was that he always ran the bases slowly, deliberately, and with his head down. Watching him circle the bases after one of his monumental home runs, it was almost as if he was apologizing for tearing the cover off of the pitcher's best pitch.

One only needs to watch a few innings of a game today to witness a home run that travels substantially less distance but nevertheless is followed first by the hitter standing in the batter's box admiring the ball until it clears the fence (this is something that I would have been benched for in Little League) and then breaking into a cocky, look-at-me, fist-pumping circling of the bases. This sometimes primitive display is usually followed by high fives to everyone but the peanut vendor and punctuated by throwing a kiss to the heavens, as if God had anything at all to do with his home run.

The problem with this egotistical display is that sports has always been a fickle lady. That same player who hit the previous home run could strike out the next two times up, including making the final out of the game with the bases loaded to lose the game. Somehow there was no dancing, fist pumping, or kiss throwing to the heavens after that last strikeout. Sometimes the distance between hero and goat is amazingly short.

There is an attitude of respect that we have somehow lost in sports, and it is particularly sad that young, impressionable children and athletes are missing that. If you love the game, love what you are doing, and respect others who love it too, then you treat it all with the respect it deserves. You don't make excuses and you realize it's not always about winning and being the hero. The very nature of winning and losing means that every contest in every sport has both a winner and a loser.

Brains versus Brawn

As luck would have it, I managed to marry into a family who had next to no knowledge of, and even less appreciation for, the game of baseball. My wife knew little about the sport, and her family knew even less. Their idea of baseball was a grown man throwing a ball at another grown man, and the latter grown man (instead of working at a real job) is supposed to hit it and run around the bases. Any feeble attempt by me to explain the complexity and the multitude of mini events going on in one particular game was like trying to describe a South Pacific sunset to a blind person.

In just about every sport you can think of, there are technical aspects that must be learned and mastered, there must be techniques practiced and refined, and there are strategies that must be learned and applied. Some of the greatest players in any sport over the years owe much of their greatness not only to their physical talents but also to their dedication and knowledge as students of the game. They study the other team, the other players, and know where they hit, how they move, and then adjust their competitive strategy based on their strengths and their weaknesses.

I'll never forget one afternoon watching baseball on television with my son Matt. During the course of the game, there was a line drive hit in the gap between center and right field, and the center fielder made an off-balance, diving, sliding, crashing, come-to-a-halt catch with most of the ball protruding from the top of the glove like a freshly scooped ice cream cone. "Wow!" Matt yelled, jumping up off the sofa. "What a catch that was!"

"It sure was!" I yelled back.

At the time, I decided to bypass a teaching moment and let him enjoy the catch. "What was the teaching moment?" you might ask. Remembering that this chapter is about both brains and brawn, let us look at another example of the lost art of brains in sports.

If we rewind the tape on the last play, I noted that the right-handed batter who hit the ball in between center and right field had been up two previous times. The first time he popped out to the second baseman, and the second time he grounded out to the first baseman.

Based on this batter's past performance, it might be safe to assume that he wouldn't pull the ball, or hit it to the left side of second base, if his life depended on it. If the center fielder had remembered where this batter has hit the ball in previous trips to the plate, he would take three or four steps toward right field when this batter first walked to the plate. Favoring the right field side of center field would have put him in a much better position to make an easier catch and be in a better position to make the throw after. No, it wouldn't have been as spectacular, but it would have been smarter.

One of the lessons I tried to instill in my teams as a coach boiled down to one rule. "Team," I would say, "if you don't remember anything else about baseball during our practices, remember this. Before every pitch in a baseball game, no matter what position you are playing, always ask yourself this question: If the ball is hit to me on this next pitch, what am I going to do with it? Where am I going to throw it? If you wait until the ball is hit to you to ask that question, it's too late!"

Being sports smart not only has to do with understanding the rules and the ins and outs of the game but also applying them in situations that are creative and sometimes out of the box.

My son Jim was playing on his middle school basketball team and enjoying an undefeated season three-quarters of the way through the schedule. Dramatically, so was the neighboring town's middle school that they had to finally play on this particular afternoon. Truth be told, the rival town's team was probably statistically better, although I will never admit to that. Surprisingly, though, Jim's team held a one-point lead with ten seconds left to go in the game. It was a tough game, and a few of our key players had already fouled out. This left our team with more inexperienced players on the court than we would have liked. I knew in the back of my mind that when we inbounded the ball, it wouldn't take the more experienced opposition much time to steal the ball, leaving enough time to score the winning basket.

What followed was one of the most incredibly creative and strategic pieces of coaching I had ever witnessed (no, I was not the coach). Knowing that we had all our timeouts remaining, the coach had one of our players pass the ball inbounds to another player and after a quick dribble called time out. Two seconds had elapsed off the ten seconds. We took our thirty-second timeout and then proceeded to inbound the ball again. Once again, a quick pass and two quick dribbles, and we called timeout again. Five seconds left! Once more we inbounded the ball and used our last timeout quickly. Three seconds left! This time, the inbound pass was thrown down underneath our own basket, which we fought to control. It didn't really matter at this point who gained possession of the ball. Despite the fact that the other team gained control of the ball, they were on the opposite end of the court with two precious seconds left. A frantic attempt to throw the ball the length of the court bounced harmlessly out of bounds, preserving our hard-fought win. Talk about winning the battle without firing a shot!

Yes, no matter what the sport, from baseball to football, basketball to tennis and golf, there is a strategy and a thought process behind the game that goes beyond the physical skills. The originators of golf didn't just put a dozen golf clubs in the golf bag to make it heavy enough to justify a golf cart. Each club performs a separate job. Each one provides a different lift or loft on the ball and subsequently a different distance that the ball can travel. This challenge is further compounded by the fact that there are other variables in the game that must be thought of before going into the bag to make a club selection. Are you on a hill, in the rough, or on the green? Does the surface pitch to the left or right? Is the grass wet or dry? Is it better to play the ball short, or lay up as the pros call it, rather than risk a longer shot that most surely will end up in the sand trap or water hazard?

If you watch a baseball game, either on television or in person, without a basic knowledge of the rules, you will miss the more exciting and important parts of the game. Without that information, it's just one grown man trying to hit a ball and another group running around chasing the ball, looking to tag the batter before he runs around completely in a circle.

In addition to the finer points of the game, other diversions are used at the ballpark to grow the interest and participation of new fans and young children. Trivia contests on the scoreboard, mascots running around the field, kids' activities between innings, and of course the ever-present concession stands and vendors hawking their wares through the stands. My father used to enjoy going to a Major League Baseball game, but as he got older and less mobile, a trip into New York to see the Yankees or Mets became harder and harder for him to tolerate. Last summer, I took him to a Bridgeport Bluefish game twenty minutes from our home. I also took my younger son John, and we arrived at the park about thirty minutes before the game.

We settled into our seats and began to watch some batting practice. There were very few people in the stadium, and it remained that way until about the second inning. By the third inning the park was full. The sellout crowd proceeded to eat everything in the ballpark, and most of the people were gone by the top of the eighth inning. It was like a huge urban block party. The food in the concession went on forever—from the traditional hot dogs and hamburgers, to nachos and egg rolls, steak bites, ice cream, popcorn, peanuts, and grilled cheese (at a baseball game?). I have been in restaurants that didn't have as varied a menu.

For the fewer but more educated fans who watched more than they ate, there seemed to be an underlying need. These fans had a need to link themselves to a team with whom they could identify. A local team provided more stability than the Major League teams now polluted with free agency and contract disputes. This was a team that didn't have 40 percent turnover rate. These fans felt more connected with the team and the players. You could actually walk down to the fence and talk to the players during batting practice or get an autograph.

These local sports franchises, no matter what sport, seem to be a way to get back to the lowest common denominator of what sports and sports fans are all about. It is a way to bring us closer to the sport and the players and narrow some of the distance that has developed through the sheer commercialization and marketing of professional sports. If you don't think that professional sports and its attitude toward its fans needs a major tune-up, consider the following.

In 1994, Major League Baseball experienced a lockout that canceled the last month and a half of the season, along with the World Series. For the first time in the modern era, there was no World Series. Previously, baseball had endured some of the most intense trials imaginable. Somehow, through World War I, the Depression, World War II, and the Korean War, baseball and the World Series lived on. During this time, it was decreed by the president himself that baseball should go on, knowing that at times it was the only thing to lift the American spirit. In 1994, because of mutual greed between the owners and the players union, they collectively took their balls and went home. In their wake, they left a nation of disappointed and outraged fans who literally paid both their salaries. We found a way to work around a world war but not a player/owner strike.

Yes, it is time to get back to what professional sports should be about. We need to pay professional athletes less and our nation's teachers more. We need to have stability where we can identify and bond with our teams and our players again. We need to bring back the opportunity to have idols that still show their boyish passion for the game. The only way I knew how to personally contribute to that goal was to become a coach.

On the surface, sports are a welcome form of diversion and recreation as we trudge through the days of our lives. It can provide a welcome method of social networking and a path to new friends and relationships. Sports can be a teacher of basic skills or a forum of interaction on how to work together for a common goal. It can teach players how to handle conflicts and provide a checklist for your own personal self-improvement. Sports can bring out the best and the worst of us.

Lately, I have gone through a transition in my attitude toward sports, which, I am ashamed to say, has come from this constant barrage of media and social pressure on winning and being number one. My son Jim recently graduated from the University of Connecticut. Given that we live only an hour from the campus, we quite naturally became fans of UConn men's and women's college basketball. In the past dozen years, the men's team has won three national championships and gone deep into postseason tournament play many other times. The women's team has won numerous national championships and enjoyed a few undefeated seasons in the past fifteen years. The women's team was instrumental in putting women's college basketball on the map.

After winning the national championship in 2011 with an unprecedented eleven-game winning run through both the Big East and NCAA tournaments, the 2012 men's team started off with a 10-1 record. During that time I found myself glued to the newspaper, television, and ESPN website following the fortunes of the team and the national rankings. As the season progressed, the Huskies went through some controversy. Some of the players were benched, the coach was reprimanded for recruiting violations, and when the dust had cleared, they had lost five of seven games. I became disappointed in myself because after this downturn into hard times, I stopped following the team in every respect. I had turned into a "fair-weather fan."

I look back now to see where this relatively new attitude might have come from. After all, I was a fan of the original Brooklyn Dodgers, whose manager, Leo Durocher, coined the phrase, "Wait till next year." I was around when the expansion team New York Mets made their entrance into Major League Baseball in 1962. The Mets compiled a first year record of 40 wins and 120 losses, and they finished tenth (last) in the National League, 60.5 games behind the NL Champion San Francisco Giants. Winning even one game was a special occasion, but they were still loveable and charismatic, and they had a huge, loyal following. It wasn't until 1969, the same year that the United States landed on the moon, that the Mets made it to and won the World Series. Unbelievable!

With a background of losing like that, you would think I would be more tolerant of a team's rough spots and rebuilding years. I asked myself, "What was the difference?" The team started off the year losing their coach on a three-game suspension for recruiting violations. A few weeks later, UConn lost one of their promising young freshmen for a three-game suspension resulting from allegedly accepting a plane ticket from university officials during his recruitment process. Incidents like these, along with free agency issues in baseball, have fragmented the concept of team in sports. I think if there was a deeper sense of team, and more longevity of players and player combinations, I could somehow get through the ups and downs of the seasons. I could enjoy the wins and appreciate the losses.

Without the sense of team that we once had, all we are left with is the desire to win. In addition, the pressure that the press and management puts on professional and college players alike to constantly win, and the pressure that parents put on their children and sports protégés to compete at a high level, strips away much of what is good and pure about sports.

Despite the ups and downs that sports has experienced over the years, no self-respecting sports fans could ever feel truly complete without trying their own hand at the sport they loved. No matter what the individual skill level and extent of sport knowledge, there is an eventual calling to be on the field, to hold the bat or the ball in your hand, to feel the sun on your face and the pounding in your chest.

It was no different for me. From the time I saw my first game on our old black-and-white, twelve-inch television screen, I knew I had to "play the game."

CHAPTER 3

Playing the Game

This chapter is a collection of individual sports memories and experiences. It is one of hundreds, thousands, dare I say it, millions of similar collections. All of these are unique to individuals and towns, throughout the country and certainly throughout the world. The collection itself, the wins, the losses, the ups and downs of all sports in which I participated, is no better or worse than all the others. The most important aspect here is that all of these experiences I have captured had a hand in planting seeds. These seeds grew into my interests, values, lessons, and prejudices that I personally developed. These sports-related experiences reinforced my interests, values, and priorities and had a significant effect on the paths taken and decisions I made in my life.

The earliest memories of my playing days go back to the driveway and front yard of our modest Cape home in Bridgeport. My first official at-bat as a four-year-old was in the driveway of that house. After drawing a replica of home plate and extending foul lines in front of the garage door, my father would help me assume the proper stance for a right-handed batter (he assumed I was not a southpaw; I would make this same assumption with my son later in life). I had a small Gil Hodges autographed bat and a white sponge rubber ball that we bought from Sam's, our local variety store down the street.

The uniform of the day made an interesting transition during this time also. I graduated from shorts, a T-shirt, and a painter's hat to a full-blown Brooklyn Dodgers uniform and cap. I even had a number on the back, which to me at five years old was pretty cool even then. My number at that time was 7; today I can tell you every player in the Dodger starting lineup at that time, and no one I can think of ever wore 7. Perhaps it was a sign of things to come. A few years later, when the Dodgers moved from Brooklyn to Los Angeles and it was impossible to see them on TV, I would switch my fan allegiance to the New York Yankees and the great #7, Mickey Mantle.

I learned to hit in the driveway, watching pitch after pitch coming from my father at the other end of the driveway. Between each pitch, and sometimes as he pitched, I would receive instruction on when to swing and to keep my eye on the ball. Gradually, I started to get the idea, and soon the ball began to fly back toward my father almost as quickly as they were thrown. My father's patience started to show through, as he spent more time running across the street after balls than actually pitching. Once I started making contact, we added the element of base running. After hitting the ball, I would joyously drop the bat and begin running around a makeshift baseball diamond we had in the front yard. What I remember most about those trips around the bases was the fact that I was running in reverse order. I would run to third, second, first, and return triumphantly to home with another home run.

Throwing and catching were also reserved for shorter periods of time devoted to dad and son, usually a few minutes before dinner. Catching a ball at five years old was not the easiest task either. Baseball gloves in the fifties were not the same technical marvels they are today. They were more padding than pocket, and you really had to use two hands to catch a ball: one hand with the glove to stop the ball and the other to squeeze the glove closed. "Use two hands!" my father would yell.

About this same time, the Cleveland Indians had a first baseman named Vic Power. Vic's claim to fame was not only being a black player in a sport still vastly dominated by white players, but he was the only player who would regularly catch a ball one handed. This truly was a phenomenon of baseball at that time. It was a novelty and something that most traditional coaches would discourage.

My glove was as sacred as anything I could imagine when it came to my favorite sport. I would hold it and look at it, pound the pocket, and enjoy the smell of the cowhide. As my friends and I got older, our actual level of skill and reputation in school was measured by the type of glove we had. Rawlings was the name that stood at the top, followed by Spaulding and some others down the line. Rawlings introduced the Trapeze six-finger glove in the early sixties, which replaced the typical webbing between the thumb and forefinger with a sixth simulated finger, which was flat. These gloves also came with model numbers that depicted the quality of the glove. The lower the number, the better the glove and the more prominent and accomplished player it signified.

I had a Rawlings TG 72, which trumped my best friend Billy's TG 78. Only Jim Riggs and Ricky Charles had lower numbers than mine, but I soon learned that there was much more to being a good baseball player than having a great glove.

The Rawlings Trapeze gloves of the sixties pale in comparison to the technological marvels of today. Today's gloves are bigger, made of synthetic material, and have pockets in which you could hide a basketball or your little sister. Many of these new gloves are black instead of the traditional cowhide brown. Seeing a black baseball glove, in this fan's opinion, is a little like seeing a fluorescent green fire truck instead of a red one. It makes my eyes roll back in my head!

School Pickup Games

As we entered school, we gradually developed a small network of classmates and friends; we also began to arrange informal games after school. Since the school was the next street over from me, I could cut though our neighbor's yard and be on the baseball diamond in the back of the school in five minutes. These games in September and from April to June at the end of the school year grew in popularity. The kids in the neighborhood all had different levels of playing ability. Some didn't even have gloves. It was not uncommon to share your glove with someone on the other team. While your team was batting, Joey or Dave would be using your glove in the outfield. When the teams changed sides they would run in and throw your glove to you and would patiently wait for his turn to bat. I remember one year, Santa Claus left me a brand-new glove under the tree on Christmas morning. Imagine my horror when the first thing my well-intentioned father did was to write my name and complete address on the thumb portion of the glove. If I had a stamp, I would have mailed the glove anywhere.

Looking back, I am amazed at how organized we were as third- and fourth-graders in scheduling and arranging these pickup games. Anyone who understands the basics of baseball realizes that you need a minimum of eight players on each side to cover all the essential positions on a baseball field. More often than not, we had six or seven players a side to play these games. That really never stopped us. If we didn't have enough players, we would close one of the outfields, for example, make right field out of bounds. If we closed right field and you hit a ball out there, you were automatically out. We didn't know this at the time, but these rules had multiple benefits. Not only did it move the game along nicely and prevent arguments, it also inadvertently taught us how to hit to a particular part of the field, which required a lot of discipline.

The real story here is that we had a solution for just about any scenario you could think of; we did not have after-school programs, soccer leagues, or T-ball. If you were younger than ten years old, Little League wasn't an option.

I hasten to add that there were *no* parents involved in these games. Ironically, the kids who did such an efficient job of facilitating these games grew up to be parents who felt that they had to plan every aspect of their child's recreational experiences.

If you are a parent, remember you don't always have to provide all the answers to your children; sometimes, instead of a fish, you can give them a fishing pole.

Street Ball

One of the great things about growing up where I did was the neighborhood. The Hooker School neighborhood of Bridgeport was built for kids to play. The houses were close together, all the same post–World War II Capes lined up together on postage stamp lots, only differentiated by their colors. The streets themselves were wide enough and relatively free of traffic. I could cut through our neighbor's yard across the street and be in Jim Riggs's backyard in thirty seconds; if I was lazy, I could stand on my front porch and watch him playing with his collie, Shadow, in his backyard. During spring and summer evenings, we had enough kids our own age within earshot to pull together a pickup game of stickball or kickball which we would play in the middle of the street.

The only drawback to these games was that the baseball diamond was almost completely in the street. Picture the following layout: If you're standing in the middle of the street looking in one direction, you were essentially standing on home plate. Somewhere to the right of you, about forty feet away in the right shoulder or gutter of the road, was first base. Farther down the street, and lined up with home plate, again in the middle of the road, was second base. Without moving from home plate, if you looked to your left, you would see third base, which was in the opposite shoulder of the road from first base, and anything beyond second base in the road was the outfield. There were usually no more than three or four kids on a side, and the challenge was to hit or kick the ball relatively straight and not hit it down the right- or left-field line. Doing so would delay the game while the outfielders had to retrieve the ball from under parked cars in driveways, under bushes, or worse yet, in Mrs. Greer's flower garden.

There were two advantages to these games. The first was that they were literally right out in front of your home. Most of the kids on the street were readily available to play. If it got dark, or your mother was yelling out the window for you, you didn't have far to go. The second, and even more wonderful, reason was Bill the ice cream man. Bill would drive his ice cream truck through the neighborhood streets at a slow and inviting speed, ringing his bell three nights during the week and on Saturday night. His 1953 Chevy truck was cleaner than most of our family cars.

Bill himself was dressed all in white, and he wore black shoes that were always shined. He had his favorite stops along each street, and when we heard the bell, the game would stop immediately. Kids of all ages would run to the truck, and parents would appear out of their houses, seemingly drawn to the truck like a magnet. We would sit at the side of the road or in someone's freshly cut lawn and enjoy our favorite ice cream. Parents actually stood around and talked as a group. It was a summertime social event that seemed to draw the entire neighborhood closer. Occasionally, Bill would learn that it was someone's birthday. If it was your birthday, your ice cream was free. He never asked for a birth certificate or driver's license, but at the same time I never knew anyone who took advantage of it.

Flash Forward

I suppose in the fast-paced world of the twenty-first century you have to wonder why I would write about something as uniquely personal and irrelevant as an after-dinner game of stickball and the ice cream man. Well, long after the game was over and we were called into the house for bath and bed, long after the ice cream was gone and wrappers thrown away, I remember what it was like on those summer evenings. The laughter, the close proximity of everything, and the friendship of the people who lived next door was all part of the fabric of the neighborhood. Parents took the time to stand around and talk together; neighbors exchanged stories, problems, concerns, and jokes. Sure we had an occasional fight, like when someone's dog got into someone else's flower bed. I guess the difference was that we had this base to fall back on. We were familiar with each other and shared our lives with each other as briefly as it was on those summer nights. When trouble happened, it was part of the territory; we resolved it, shook hands, and moved on.

Today, I live in a cul-de-sac on a quiet street. I can honestly say, as outgoing and friendly as I think I am, I only know about 10 percent of my neighbors on the street. I don't mean that I haven't met them; I mean I couldn't even tell you what they looked like if I passed them in the grocery store. I am sure we are all good people, basically friendly, with no axes to grind, yet I don't know them. We don't have an opportunity to get to know each other, to talk, to share even superficially about the weather or last night's game.

Once or twice a week, I go over to my son Matt's house and pick up his dogs. The dogs, twin boxers about five years old, are named Buddy and Betty, or as I affectionately refer to them, Nit and Wit. I pick them up because they live in a fairly populated area and don't get the chance to run around much. I bring them over to my ample yard, where we proceed to run around until we all collapse in a heap on the lawn from exhaustion.

Anyway, one day we were in the yard, running around, kicking the soccer ball, trying to keep Betty from eating it, when I looked up to see a car coming down the street. I looked up and thought I recognized the car, so I smiled and waved. As the car got a little closer, I realized that the driver was not the person I thought it was. When he saw me wave, he looked over at me, confused. I could tell by his blank expression that I was not someone in his memory database. Having decided I was not on his list of friends and acquaintances, he drove by without returning a wave or even a smile.

I guess I must have missed the memo that said that "You need to know someone before you are allowed to wave to them." As I raised my three boys, I often repeated the following advice. If you have children, or even if you are one, remember the three most important things to do every day:

1. Make a new friend.

2. Learn something new.

3. Have a nice lunch.

If you can accomplish those three things every day, you'll have a good day, and if you drive by my house, it's okay to wave!

Cub Scout Softball

Outside of elementary school recess, my first experience with adult-supervised sports was in my first year of Cub Scouts. One spring evening at our monthly scout pack meeting, the den leaders decided to initiate a softball league by dividing up the pack into six teams to play each other during the spring and early summer months. Looking back on this effort, after years of organizing similar leagues as an adult and father, I applaud our scout leaders for this effort. The first order of business at the pack meeting that night was to pass out index cards with pencils. We were all instructed to write down the position that we would prefer to play in a softball game.

I knew all the positions, of course, and probably by then had played them all in pickup games after school. One of the truths about youth activities is that scouting tends to draw the quieter, less confident, and less athletic boys than other more sports-minded activities. Case in point: Bruce Scholer's index card simply announced his position preference as "batter." I am not sure how much behind the scenes sorting there was after the cards were passed in, but eventually six fairly well-balanced teams emerged.

The interesting thing about these teams was that my more athletically inclined friends were not involved in scouting. The result was a different mix of skills and personalities than I was used to. One of my good friends in school was Jim Riggs, who arguably was the best athlete in the school. Part of the reason he was so good was because he associated with friends who were two to three years older than he was. Because I hung around with him, I had the same exposure. That meant as third- and fourth-graders, Jimbo and I were playing baseball and football with fifth- and sixth-graders. If you want to get better in anything, you need to compete with people who are better than you are. Sometimes you come away from this type of competition battered and bloody, but I have found that it raises the bar on your performance very quickly.

After the scout league began, I grew to really look forward to Monday nights in the schoolyard. Bringing my glove to a scout meeting and not having to wear the scout uniform were interesting diversions to the regularly held scout meetings. I got to play first base, my preferred position, which was played by another one of my idols, Brooklyn Dodger Gil Hodges. As I played more, it became obvious to teammates and scout leaders that I was the fastest scout in our eighty-member pack. At the Cub Scout Blue and Gold picnic of 1961, we competed in a 100-yard dash. All the scouts lined up and proceeded to run the race. I came in first out of everyone, to my amazement.

Also at the Blue and Gold picnic, I teamed up with my best friend, Billy, for the wheelbarrow races. Billy and I took first place in that event as well. The prize for first place was a Wiffle ball set, which included a black plastic bat and four new Wiffle balls. The prize for winning the 100-yard dash was another Wiffle ball set: a black plastic bat and four new Wiffle balls. You don't have to have a degree in inventory control to realize that we had two brand-new bats and eight new balls. After that, Billy and I began an entertaining, competitive, and well-thought-out two-people Wiffle ball league.

Baseball Cards

If Cub Scout softball, pickup games at school, Little League, tackle football at the park, and church league basketball were the bricks of my lifelong sports experiences, then my baseball card collection was the mortar that held those bricks together. I actually started collecting baseball cards at the age of five, when I could hardly read what was on them. They were an exciting extension of connecting with baseball and the men that played the game. At first, the cards had illustrations rather than actual photographs. They were usually a headshot of the player with a superimposed action shot of them sliding, throwing, hitting, or otherwise looking like a hero.

Baseball cards had many purposes. I guess the primary purpose was in trading them, flipping for them, and otherwise collecting them. The cards were released in sets and had numbers on the back. They came in packs of five or six cards with a stick of pink bubble gum in the pack. The gum always gave the cards a remarkably wonderful smell, and sometimes the sugar from the gum stuck on the cards to give them an added texture that was either welcome or not, depending on what they were used for. I kept my cards in a shoebox, arranged either numerically, according to the checklists, or in teams, which was my preference later on.

These cards were keepsakes, and we kept close tabs on the cards we had and the cards we needed to fill out a set by meticulously checking off the boxes next to each individual's name on the series checklist. There were usually seven series of cards with about seventy to eighty cards in each series. As the spring and summer weeks wore on, those of us serious collectors would keep track of which stores had which series. If you bought a pack from an unfamiliar store, you ran the risk of getting doubles. On the other hand, if you stopped by a store that just received the next series of cards fresh off the press, you could be assured that all cards in each pack were new additions to your growing collection.

To kids who were not serious collectors, these cards were much less important. Younger siblings of card collectors, especially little sisters, found it particularly amusing to clip baseball cards to the spokes of their bicycle wheels. As they rode their bike down the street, the cards would be slapped by the spokes as they rode, making a clicking sound. I guess it was supposed to make the bike sound like it had a motor. Once a baseball card was used for this purpose, it was virtually useless for anything else. The picture was marred beyond recognition, and the statistics on the back were completely illegible. There was nothing more discouraging than seeing one of the cards you plotted all summer to get flapping away on the spokes of little sister Mary's pink tricycle. It was enough to make a ten-year-old boy go mad.

I started collecting cards in the late 1950s, but I wasn't serious about collecting until a year or two later.

At one point, I arranged my cards according to my favorite teams, but when the Dodgers departed to the West Coast, I was stuck for new idols. This was when I forged my boyhood allegiance with Mickey Mantle. The high point of the 1960 baseball card season was finding one of Mickey's cards. That year, it seemed that every other pack I opened had a Dave Nicholson card in it. I only saw one Mickey Mantle card.

I bought that hallowed pack on the way back to school after lunch. I immediately wanted to take it home and protect it at all costs, but I would never make it back to school on time. Because our school had a firm rule about bringing cards into the classroom, I snuck the card into my geography book to keep it clean and safe and to protect it from my greedy classmates. By the end of the day, I was firmly convinced that teachers and students alike could somehow see through the top of my desk and through the cover of my geography book; I imagined they knew what treasure lay hidden underneath. I was sure that suspicion would be aroused when I took my geography book home on a night when there was no geography homework. I did get a smile and some brownie points from Miss Blake that day. That was the longest afternoon of my young life.

One day after school, Carl Demery, a large, intimidating card collector, was to teach me the finer points of card flipping. By the time the lesson was over, I had been cleaned out of about 70 percent of my collection. I was not only devastated but way too embarrassed to tell anyone about it. The plus side of this degrading experience was that in addition to baseball cards, Topps also produced football cards. The format was the same, and I was able to start the same process with Frank Gifford and Johnny Unitas.

I started collecting football cards at an even faster pace. I quickly filled another shoebox and had most of the players on most of the teams. In addition to their educational and aesthetic value, I also used these cards to conduct simulated football games, pitting one team against another. I would lay on the floor and manipulate the cards, passing, throwing, and tackling in some arbitrary random fashion that produced unpredictable scores. I even went as far as creating my own football field, covering a large piece of cardboard with green paper. I put stripes and hash marks on the field using a ruler. I even placed colored stars in the end zones. It truly was ingenious. As I look back on this solitary, manual pastime, I have to laugh to myself. With today's PCs, DVDs, and PlayStations, there is no need for this type of primitive play. Madden Football has filled the void, taking all the thought and creativity out of the game.

This new direction in card collecting was enough to take the sting out of losing most of my baseball cards to Carl. I vowed I would never be duped like that again. I started by eliminating card flipping as a method of growing (or depleting) my inventory.

As my friends and I gathered more cards, we also refined our card collecting strategies. As the summer wore on, the next series would come out and the previous series would kind of purge itself off the shelves and become harder to find. Billy and I found out, by accident, that if you expanded your geographic area of card collecting, you might find an out-of-the-way store in a neighboring town that had cards from first and second series, even though the fourth series was out.

Another card collecting strategy was in the selection of the packs. We are not talking about picking up an arbitrary pack of gum or cigarettes here. This was an act to be carefully thought out and savored. Twenty-five cents would get you five packs of baseball cards. The cards came in boxes containing three rows of ten packs. In order to get the best packs with the best quality cards, there were two critical rules to follow.

1. First, never take a pack from the top of the pile. Doing so will almost guarantee that every card in that pack will be a double of players you already have.

2. Second, if you are buying more than one pack, never take both packs from the same row of cards in the box. Later, as an adult, I learned that this selection process was an accepted quality-control standard of random sampling.

If nothing else, these rules proved that sports fans, especially baseball fans, are very superstitious creatures. During the 1961 and '62 seasons, Topps baseball cards also added baseball stamps and coins to the packs. The stamps actually came with a book; you could put the stamps in the book and watch your collection grow by teams. I guess these additions were intended to make trading more attractive, but the cards and stamps never had much of a function or draw for my friends and me.

The Card Collectors' Company

The spring of 1961 brought new changes and new attitudes. One of the strategic changes that boosted the quality of my baseball card collection, ironically enough, was Cub Scouts. Yes, the same group who introduced me to my first real organized team sport. Cub Scouts traditionally received a monthly magazine called *Boys Life*. As a Cub or Boy Scout, you could always count on your monthly publication to give you the blueprints for a bird house or show how to keep your supply of food away from the bears on your next camping trip. In the back of the magazine were advertisements on everything from Indian lore to the best summer camps at Lake Wachamogo.

One day, as I flipped through the pages of these breathtaking features, I happened upon a small ad for an outfit in upstate New York called the Card Collectors' Company. Very simply, you could pull out any Topps baseball card checklist and write down the numbers of any cards in that series that you were missing. You merely submitted those numbers, along with a check or money order for the total (approximately a nickel apiece for the cards you were ordering). The Card Collectors' Company would mail you brand-new cards (sans bubble gum) in a brown envelope. Just think of it! Never again were you at the mercy of the random pack of bubble gum cards. Yes, I could still buy my packs at Sam's or the Beardsley Pharmacy, but I had a hidden insurance policy that no matter what, at the end of the day, I would have all the cards in each of the seven series. You would have this assurance without the additional inconvenience of having to buy pack after pack of doubles and triples of the same card to get the final card in the set.

During this season, Billy and I quickly amassed the most complete set of baseball cards in the history of card collecting. Further, we arranged them into teams and positions in such a fashion that the Dewey Decimal System would be envious. We could pull out complete teams with pitching rosters at a moment's notice. This was especially gratifying since 1961 was the expansion year. The American and National Leagues both expanded by two new teams. The American League added the Los Angeles Angels and the Minnesota Twins, and the National League added the New York Mets and the Houston Colt .45s. I was about to add that the Minnesota Twins was actually not the new team but the old established Washington Senators that picked up and moved to Minnesota. The new expansion team was the Washington Senators who eventually became the Texas Rangers. Yes, I believe we went around that same block earlier in the book, but I figured that the absurdity of the whole thing was worth repeating.

There was another blessing for which I was forever in debt to the Cub Scouts. Earlier, I shared the exciting story of our success at the Blue and Gold picnic. With my speed and the teamwork between Billy and myself, we managed to bring home two Wiffle ball bats and eight Wiffle balls. This ample inventory, along with our tremendously well-organized baseball card resource, became the ingredients for our positively awesome and authentic two-player Wiffle ball league.

Billy and I had all the natural resources we needed to start what was to be a pretty amazing likeness of a professional baseball league. We certainly had the personnel. Thanks to our comprehensive baseball card collection, we had more than five hundred cards arranged by team and league in a large shoebox. The team cards preceded all the individual cards and were staggered in the box so that they protruded out like file tabs in a drawer. This made finding any team an easy task.

As for the equipment, we both had our Little League Rawlings Trapeze gloves, and we also had our Wiffle ball bats and balls. The only other item we needed was a pad and pencil, which eventually turned into an actual baseball scorebook. We could write in lineups and keep an inning-by-inning account of what happened in the game. Scorekeeping, by the way, was a skill that we both learned our first year in Little League. Wiffle ball really gave us a chance to hone that skill under game conditions.

Finding a location for the games wasn't a problem. We both had very similar yards and houses. We would play in the driveway, pitching up against the garage door, sometimes to our fathers' dismay. The garage doors had a series of boxes painted white. Two of those boxes became home plate, depending on whether the hitter was right or left handed.

At the time, Wiffle ball for two eleven-year-olds was just a natural extension of the sport that we loved. Looking back as an adult, I recognize what an exercise it was in developing physical and mental skills along with creativity, problem solving, innovation, and independent thinking. This was another example of how much we could accomplish without any adult supervision.

In addition to keeping score, we also added another challenge to the game. We each chose a team from the box of baseball cards to play on any given day. From the twenty or so individual cards that were on each team, we would select a lineup and a pitcher along with some backup pitchers for relief. We put the cards in the order they would be batting and proceeded with the game. The real challenge for two natural right-handed hitters was that we had to bat either left handed or right handed, depending on who was up and what the back of the card said. At first batting left handed for either one of us was almost a sure strikeout. Gradually, as we played more games, Billy and I both became very proficient at hitting lefty or righty.

Coincidentally, this first year of our Wiffle ball league was our first year of Little League. These two events happened so close together that we actually came back from our opening day events of Mass, parade, and exhibition game and had our first Wiffle ball game in my driveway that afternoon.

We were so excited to keep playing that we kept our Little League uniforms on as we headed out to the driveway. Billy and I skimmed through the teams, deciding who the first two teams on opening day should be; we looked up at each other and laughed. Billy had his St. Louis Cardinal uniform on, and I had my San Francisco Giants uniform. This was a no-brainer!

The first Wiffle ball game of the new season would be the Giants and the Cardinals.

May 6, 2012, was the fiftieth anniversary of that game. As though the game was yesterday, I can still remember my lineup:

Giants Lineup

1. Jose Pagan SS

2. Chuck Hiller 2B

3. Willie McCovey RF

4. Willie Mays CF

5. Orlando Cepeda 1B

6. Harvey Kuenn 3B

7. Joe Amalfitano LF

8. Ed Bailey C

9. Juan Marichal P

Billy's lineup had many of the St. Louis stars of the late 1950s and early '60s, including Stan Musial, Tim McCarver, Ken Boyer, Curt Flood, Dal Maxvill, and his ace pitchers Bob Gibson and Bob Duliba. On this particular day, the pitching matchup was Bob Duliba for the Cardinals and the high-kicking Dominican Juan Marichal for the Giants.

It was the afternoon of that same beautiful day that greeted us for the opening ceremonies at the Park City Little League field. Some of that celebration and fanfare seemed to spill over into our game. Through the first three innings, there was no score, and in the eighth inning, the score still stood at Cardinals 0, Giants 0. Both pitchers ended the regulation with a scoreless tie and over ten strikeouts apiece. There was never a real threat at any one time, mostly a single or two and an occasional walk, but nothing that mounted a serious threat.

The afternoon dragged on, and we made it through the eleventh, the thirteenth, and onto the fifteenth inning. I was batting in the bottom of the fifteenth and had already gone through the heavy hitters in the previous inning. The bottom of the order was coming up, and we were both starting to consider changing pitchers. Harvey Kuenn started the inning by grounding out. The next batter was the unremarkable left fielder for the Giants, Joey Amalfitano. He was your average outfielder, certainly not with the credentials of Mays and McCovey. Joey did manage to meet the second pitch to him and sent a hard line drive over the fence for a walk-off home run. Giants 1, Cardinals 0. The first Wiffle Ball League game was in the books.

As the summer approached and school let out, the games were more frequent and organized. Sometimes we played double headers. We became better at switch hitting, and the games started to generate more offense. We actually had a home-run race. Games would alternate between Billy's house and mine. Although similar in many respects, both driveway stadiums had their challenges and differences, just like two different golf courses. Billy's yard had an enormous maple tree, which served as first base and the right-field line. The branches hung out far enough to block the view of right field.

A Taste of the Major Leagues

As we continued to play, we continued to refine the game and the league. Billy and I created standings and eventually kept some basic statistics. We picked All-Star teams and had two games. At the end of the season, American and National League champions were declared and our first World Series was played. The Series would pit the Milwaukee Braves against the Baltimore Orioles. The Braves eventually beat the Orioles in a thrilling seven-game Series. Lew Burdette and Warren Spahn were the ace pitchers for the Braves, and Milt Papas and Chuck Estrada pitched for the Orioles.

During our second summer, I attended a New York Mets baseball game and came home with a realistic-looking batting helmet that we also made part of the game. There is probably no functional reason for protective headgear in a game that is played with a plastic ball full of holes, but it looked real, and we felt like a Major Leaguer when we were wearing it in the batter's box.

The most significant and impressive addition to our Wiffle ball league was the scoreboard. Previously we had kept score and statistics in an actual scorebook. What better way to add a sense of Major League ballpark realism than to build a miniature replica of a Major League manual scoreboard? Now, for this undertaking, you would want a good model to follow, and my motivation for this was the huge scoreboard in right center field of Yankee Stadium.

The scoreboard had everything: the inning-by-inning totals of runs, hits, and errors and each team's lineup. Now, during these golden years of sports, there were no fifty-foot-high color images of your favorite player with his name and statistics emblazoned underneath for the entire world to see. In the individual team lineup on the scoreboard, there was a uniform number and a position. For example, if you looked in the first slot of the Yankee lineup on the scoreboard, you would see a #1 and underneath it the designation 2B. Next position was #10 at SS and #9 RF, and so on. Unless you were from a distant planet you knew that on that day, Bobby Richardson was leading off and playing second base, Tony Kubek was at shortstop, and Roger Maris was batting third and in right field, and so on.

If the Cleveland Indians were in town, and you were less familiar with their lineup, you would only need to refer to your fifty-cent program, which listed all the teams and all the uniform numbers.

The Yankee Stadium scoreboard also had another feature. It actually posted all the games in the American and National League that were scheduled that day. It would have the team names, the score, the inning number, and the two pitchers in the game at that time. Anyway, back to Wiffle ball.

With the vision of that monumental scoreboard etched in my mind, I set out to create a replica for our Wiffle ball games. I tracked down a piece of clean plywood, about three and a half feet square. I then cut thin three-inch by one-half-inch pinstripes that were nailed in place to create a line of ten slots for home and visiting team. It included a larger slot for team name and then inning slots, one through seven, and the last three for runs, hits, and errors. Underneath, it repeated the same process with smaller slots to create the American and National League schedule and score updates. Using letter and number stencils, I painstakingly traced team names and a large variety of numbers on white cardboard. I colored in the background of all the letters and numbers with black marker, leaving the letters and numbers white. In my mind this simulated the lighted numbers on the scoreboard. Each team name and individual number was cut out neatly and placed into a box with a lid.

On game day, we would bring the scoreboard out and set it up on Mr. Erst's stone wall down the third-base line, in clear view of Billy and me and any passersby. As the game progressed, we would fish out the appropriate numbers from the box and place them on the scoreboard. It was truly the crowning touch.

Mary's Gift Shop

The more realistic we made this league, the more we wanted to play and the number of games increased. With school out and the summer vacation in full swing, Billy and I had plenty of time to play and refine the rules and conditions of the league. We played so much at this point that the games were starting to take its toll on the equipment. Our two original black plastic bats were starting to get worn and cracked. Black electrical tape worked well for a while and then failed. We invested in a new bat that was plastic but thinner and yellow instead of black. The thinner bat made the games a little more challenging, but it was a welcome change. We also found a great supplier for new Wiffle balls. Mary's Gift Shop was a small musty store that had a little bit of everything in it. It was, in my mind, a tag sale with a door. Mary was also old and musty but sweet as pie with her curly gray, close-cropped hair and her little spectacles that she peered over whenever she heard the ringing of the bell tied over the top of her door.

Although Billy and I only went in there for Wiffle balls, it was fun to browse through all the eclectic toys and gifts that she had strewn around her old shop. When it came time to make our purchase, we would put the balls on the counter and hand Mary a few dollar bills. She didn't have a cash register but she did have an old box with some coins, old buttons, and possibly a safety pin or two. She would painstakingly search through the box, always coming up with the right change. She would then take a brown paper bag and slowly and deliberately slide the purchase into the bag and staple it neatly, as if to protect the treasure inside. As a twelve-year-old, I never could figure out why she took so much time and care in packing up a few plastic balls. As I look back on her as an adult, it was painfully obvious that she just didn't want us to leave. If we had stayed a little longer, she probably would have served us chocolate pudding. Thank you, Mary . . . God bless you.

Night Games

Believe it or not, there was more to my life as a boy than just sports. I had also started to develop an interest in, and eventually a love for, photography. My father shared that interest, and we were able to create a great little darkroom in our cellar to develop black-and-white negatives and prints. Although I could write another book on photography, the most relevant part of this experience was that my father and I had acquired two floodlights for photography. The bulbs created a tremendous amount of light, and with two eight-inch reflectors, they could throw light over a large area. The floodlights also had a pinch grip on the stem that allowed them to be secured to just about any surface.

One night, Billy and I were playing the second game of a double header and were rapidly running into dusk. In the rapidly fading daylight, Billy quipped, "It's too bad we don't have lights." Then my own personal lights went on. "Hold on," I said. I ran into the house and returned a few minutes later with the two floodlights, some extension cords, and a small step ladder. In a matter of minutes, we had a surprisingly well-lit stadium to continue playing. With strategic placement and aim, the two floodlights covered the entire driveway, the scoreboard, and just about the entire street to the lawn directly across from us. The only problem was that a fly ball disappeared from view for a while, but nothing in life is perfect. Just when we thought we couldn't expand our capabilities any more, we added an entire schedule of night games.

The lights were also good marketing. Neighbors would come to their doors at night out of curiosity. Passersby would stop to watch a few pitches. The occasional car that would drive by would slow and sometimes stop, assuming it was an accident scene or a police safety checkpoint.

We had great fun, and I have warm memories from those summers with a seemingly unimportant plastic bat and ball. How could something so overlooked by most create such an opportunity for two friends to bond, to explore innovation and imagination, and to create a fun and harmless pastime for the summer? From home-run races to World Series play and even a perfect game, which Billy pitched one summer night, it seemed as though this fun and amusement would go on forever. The league was also very exclusive. We never let any of our many friends into this hallowed league. Yes, we all played Wiffle ball to some degree together, but no one but us entered into the inner sanctum of our league.

It's hard to believe the league lasted four summers, from 1962 to 1966. Even as high school sophomores, Billy and I continued to play into the summer months. It was as if time had stood still and we were still twelve-year-old Little Leaguers. But one night in the middle of a game, we had to stop play quickly to let a car go by. The car was driven by Ray, a high school classmate. He was dropping my sister off after cheerleader practice at the high school, and in the car were two other cheerleaders that lived close by. The girls waved and laughed, seeing Billy and me playing with what seemed to be kid's toys.

As the car pulled away, Billy and I looked at each other; it was a moment I will never forget. It was as if we had been walking around naked but never thought anything of it until someone confronted us. Instantly we could feel our nakedness; we felt how embarrassingly juvenile we must have looked to our peers. It was worse to think that they were girls, who were always worthy of our most impressive side. All of a sudden the interest and the passion were gone. It was apparently time to put away the bats and plastic balls, the scoreboard, and the baseball cards. I don't remember many more games after that night. The new school year was upon us, and we were engulfed with academics and high school sports.

The following spring, the new baseball cards came out. Out of sheer habit, we went down to Sam's to buy the first few packs of the year. The cards seemed cheaper and not well done. We only collected a few packs before baseball card collecting faded into nothing. It was the same year the Yankees moved Mickey Mantle from center field to first base. What was happening all of a sudden?

I look back on those days of Wiffle ball and baseball cards and wonder what it would have been like if Billy and I hadn't been left to our own resources. Would it have been better to have our fathers help and encourage us, or were we better off the way we were, two friends trying to simulate the Major Leagues all by themselves? I wonder if, as a parent, I could have resisted the temptation to jump into a similar situation with my children, uninvited, and start building the scoreboard or hanging the lights.

Hold on to sixteen as long as you can, changes come around real soon make us women and men.

—John Mellencamp

Jim Chernesky

Kickball: Making a Name at Hooker School

Nestled in the middle of our normal school day, somewhere between reading, spelling, math, and social studies, was a twenty-five-minute recess period. Twenty-five minutes can be an eternity in the dentist's chair, but it goes by fairly quickly when trying to play any type of team sport. Baseball in twenty-five minutes is highly improbable, not to mention the added pressure of remembering bats, balls, and gloves. One of the ways we could enjoy all the benefits of baseball without inhaling was to play kickball during recess. Kickball uses the same playing field, basic rules, scoring, and team logistics as baseball. The most significant difference is the baseball is replaced with an inflated ball about the same size of a basketball. It is rolled from the pitcher's mound toward home plate. You stand about six to eight feet behind home plate, and as the ball is rolled toward you, you take a few well-timed steps and attempt to kick the ball in the same general area as you would hit a baseball. One of the "nice to haves" in the game is an asphalt surface or at least a very level surface. Bumps, weeds, and rocks along the ball's path can make for a very erratic pitch, and if you take your eyes off the unpredictable path of the ball, you could find yourself kicking at air and winding up on your backside.

One other interesting twist to this game is something called the mound rule. If you kick the ball to the second basemen, he or she has an option: either throwing it to the first basemen, who tags the runner or steps on first to get the hitter out, or throwing the ball to the pitcher, who is standing on the pitcher's mound. The pitcher simply tags the pitcher's mound while holding the ball, and if done before the batter gets to first base, the batter is out. Another way this rule is used is that if batter, for example, kicks the ball and is circling the bases when the ball is finally relayed into the pitcher standing on the pitcher's mound, the base runner has to return to his or her previous base (unless more than halfway to the next base).

Because these games were played almost daily as part of the normal school day, they could, if necessary, be a continuation that stretched over the course of a few days. They became a kind of sports-recreational soap opera. The other aspect of these games that we figured out was finding ways to limit the logistical side of the game so that we could use as much of those actual twenty-five minutes playing the game rather than sifting through the administrative tasks. That meant teams were chosen and batting orders were confirmed ahead of time. We only needed one ball, so equipment was not an issue. These were not teacher rules, and the game wasn't parent instigated or supervised; it was just another example of hit the ground running planning and implementation by fourth-, fifth-, and sixth-graders.

Based on my preestablished ability for speed and my ever-developing baseball skills, I quickly became one of the three top threats in this sport on the Thomas Hooker playground. This honor, bestowed by my classmates, was especially gratifying since many times these games were coed. The fact that Kathy or Beverly couldn't wait until it was my turn to be in the batter's box did nothing but reinforce my quiet confidence on the field and off.

We kept records too, which was a double-edged sword. Even at the tender age of twelve, I realized that these public statistical displays were only welcome if you were on or near the top of that list. I was happy with my own accomplishments but felt bad for those who had all they could do to meet ball with foot. By the time we worked our way through the middle grades to the junior high grades of seventh and eighth grade, kickball was replaced by softball.

Another Milestone

My sixth-, seventh-, and eighth-grade years also coincided with my years in Little League. There were really four of us who played Little League ball and, as such, stood out considerably from the pack when playing softball on the playground during gym period.

One of my most memorable experiences in gym softball came on the very last day of school in 1964. We had finished our classes and passed our books in. Eighth grade graduation in the gym was only a few days away before we went our separate ways, to high school and beyond. I could feel the finality of these days as we prepared to play our last softball game. The weather that summer was warm with tree buds well on their way to being full foliage. It felt more like summer vacation than a school day.

These eighth-grade games were a bit more orderly than in previous years because the gym teacher, Mr. Garret, pitched for both sides and umpired the games, which made the outcomes a bit more even. We were three-quarters of the way through the game and I had one, maybe two more at-bats before this chapter of my life was over. I stepped to the plate with one runner on second base and looked out over the playground; Mr. G was prepared to deliver the underhanded pitch. The playground itself went on forever outside the stretches of the left and center fielder, only interrupted by a basketball court with two poles and backboards in dead left field. Right center field and right field, however, were framed by the face of the school's auditorium, rising up about forty feet from the pavement. The last twenty feet to the roof was lined with a series of huge paned windows. The windows reflected the near noon day sun on a cloudless day.

Mr. G, normally an accurate pitcher, seemed to be getting tired, and his first pitch was inside and high, close to my left ear. I let it go. The next pitch came in approximately the same place, and I swung impatiently. The pitch trailed off in back of me, foul. Mr. G adjusted his position a little and delivered the next pitch, which came in about head-high on the outside corner of the plate. I stepped into the pitch, just trying to hit it where it was, and not looking to hit it to left field.

When you don't catch the ball full on the bat, especially on a cold day, you get a cracking sound of the bat and sometimes even a buzzing that will sting your hands. Sometimes, however, you hit the ball so squarely on the bat, so hard, that you hardly feel the impact. This was one of those times. The ball seemed to explode off my bat and headed in a high arc toward right center field. At first I thought it would just be a fly ball that would be caught by the center fielder. As I ran toward first, I looked up again and saw the ball was still going up and headed for the auditorium. I was taught to never stop running on the base path and always watch the coaches. But in this case, I slowed almost to a stop to watch what was about to happen. The ball slammed into one of the twenty-foot window frames about three-quarters of the way up, about ten feet from the roof of the auditorium. The ball hit two and a half of the smaller panes of glass that made up the window, and a shower of glass, plaster, and paint rained down on the playground.

I circled the bases, remembering how Mickey Mantle would do it in a monumental moment such as this: with his head down. I could feel the embarrassment, not of breaking the window (which, during a gym period, wasn't a billable item), but for doing something extraordinary in the face of my teammates and friends.

After the period was over, Mr. G wished us all well and hoped to see us around the high school circuit. As we dispersed for the last time, he called Jim Riggs and me over to speak to us privately. He took us aside one on one. I figured he wanted to get my address so my parents could pay for the window. He told me that he was selected as an administrator of physical education for the new high school in Trumbull, Connecticut. He was offering me a full four-year scholarship to this private Catholic high school. He told us that we would be a valuable addition to their sports program.

As an eighth-grader you can't grasp the significance of an offer like that. I always assumed I was going to Warren Harding High School. It was a school steeped in tradition academically, and its athletic program was recognized throughout the state. My father had graduated from Harding in 1944. My cousin Mike was quarterback of the football team in the early 1950s, going undefeated in his senior year. Of course I was going to Harding! This was an easy choice, and I didn't even tell my parents about the offer. I went on to Harding and on with the rest of my life.

You have to wonder, though, at these crossroads of your life how different things could have been, for better or for worse, with each of these decisions. The people you would meet, the places you would go, experiences, opportunities, and challenges. Sometimes, when you are confronted with these decisions, you take your best shot with what you know and what you believe. In the movie *Bagger Vance*, Will Smith is a caddy who tells his golfer this unforgettable line: "Listen to your heart. Your heart is smarter than your head/ hands are ever going to be."

Little League Baseball

Bull Durham is a great movie with Kevin Costner and Susan Sarandon. It's a story about an aging minor league baseball catcher who has always dreamed of making it to the Major Leagues and his struggles to get there. He refers to that final leap to the big leagues as going to "the Show." For me, making the team and participating in Little League was "the Show." Wearing that uniform and being on the field with green grass, white lines, and rosin bags on the pitcher's mound was better than all the school pickup games and Cub Scout softball games put together.

After the obligatory registrations and meetings, the day finally came for tryouts for the Park City Little League. For a while, there was some confusion over whether I could even participate because of where we lived and how we fit into the district. The first day of tryouts finally came, and I found myself along with a small army of other eleven- and twelve-year-old hopefuls one early and chilly morning in April at Beardsley Park. Wearing sweatshirts and whatever type of baseball cap we had around the house, we lined up and dutifully took turns running through all types of drills, which demonstrated our running, throwing, catching, and hitting. We would wait nervously in line until it was our turn to perform and then hope we were able to pull together our best effort. Every time we finished our assigned drill, we would glance over to one of the many coaches standing on the sidelines while they wrote intently on their clipboard.

You would think that at the end of a stressful day of being tested mentally and physically, you would be put out of your misery with some sort of decision on your fate. Even if it was bad news, at least you would know. This was not to be, however, and the tryouts lasted another two sessions on different days at different locations. The final tryout session was held on the actual Little League field. The league officials thanked us for our participation and told us we would be notified soon of the results.

The next few days, I waited patiently by the mailbox for some official news of whether or not I was going to "the Show." One night, around dinnertime, after the mailman had disappointed me once again, the phone rang. My mother answered the phone and after a few "yes" responses and a faint smile, she turned to me and said, "That was your Little League coach. You have practice on Saturday morning at ten o'clock." The joy and excitement I felt was indescribable, but it was mixed with a little disappointment that there wasn't more fanfare in this momentous announcement.

There was plenty of fanfare, however, on opening day. In May 1962, we had all received our uniforms and mimeographed instructions on what time to report for opening day festivities. We all met early on a Saturday morning right before Memorial Day in the basement of St. Charles Church. The day kicked off in the morning with a forty-five-minute Mass upstairs in the church. Either 95 percent of the league was Roman Catholic, or I had somehow missed the memo on where to be. I spent the duration of the Mass downstairs in the church hall, playing tag with two Jewish players and three

Baptists. Toward the end of the Mass, you could smell coffee and bacon and the sound of dishes and silverware rattling in the larger room adjacent to us.

After a wholesome breakfast and a few speeches, we filed out of the church and marched down East Main Street; a police escort led us up East Main to Boston Avenue and then past Lakeview Cemetery. As we turned onto Asylum Street, I could see the large flag, the Stars and Stripes, gently twisting in the warm spring air. As we marched closer, I could hear the snapping of the multicolored triangular plastic pennants that surrounded the field. This truly was a day I would never forget.

The entire league marched onto the field, assorted neatly by teams, all standing in straight rows. After the playing of the national anthem, we all dispersed into the bleachers, along with parents and friends, to watch a series of two-inning exhibition games.

Our game was the third in a series of six, and it seemed forever until we made it onto the field. I was batting sixth and playing second base. As I stood on the freshly manicured field and stared down at the batter, the catcher, and the umpire, it truly seemed like a dream. The dream came to an abrupt end when the crack of the bat brought me back to earth. I looked up to see a brand-new Rawlings Little League baseball hopping toward me at a fast pace. *This is it!* I thought. *My first play, my first chance in the Show!* I shuffled a few steps to my right and the ball hit my glove. "Two hands," I could hear my father say, and I grabbed the ball. I had plenty of time to make the play, but I wanted to get it over with. I threw the ball awkwardly across my body to the first baseman, who at this point wasn't all that far away. "Yer out!" I heard the umpire bark. I looked up to see where my parents were sitting, but there were too many people in the bleachers. *There, that wasn't so bad,* I thought. *You are now a veteran.*

Rookie Year with the Giants

My initial fear about not being in the right district to play Little League baseball was clarified at this point. There were actually two districts. My district was the National League, which was comprised of the Dodgers, Cardinals, Braves, and my Giants. Somehow, fate had prevented me from becoming one of my beloved Dodgers, but at this point the San Francisco Giants were an acceptable substitute. As it turned out, it was going to be the difference between first and last place, but more on that later.

As the season got under way, I started to develop a sense of team for the first time in my playing experience. We had two great coaches, John Stott and Cliff Richards. Coach Stott was a gray-haired grandfather type who was soft spoken and wise but could grill you like a hot dog if you failed to meet his expectations. Coach Stott did not have a son in the league. He had no hidden agenda on why he was coaching or who he was secretly trying to promote. Later, as an adult and a coach myself, I was hard pressed to ever find someone who coached a sport strictly for the love of the game and to pass on his knowledge and passion. Coach Stott had more than a little influence on my decision to coach and share what I knew and experienced.

Coach Richards, his assistant, looked like a cross between Casey Stengel and Popeye the sailor. He had that sunken toothless jaw look and an intensity that was younger than his years. Coach Richards always gave the second part of the pregame pep talk to the team and often expelled a little gas at the conclusion of his words of wisdom. This would always send the entire dugout into waves of snickers and laughs. To this day, I wonder if he did it intentionally, just to break the pregame jitters. He always brought an entire box of Beechnut Fruit Stripe gum and left it on the top shelf in the dugout. Funny the things that sticks in your mind fifty years later.

As a rookie, I only played two innings during the first part of the season. Two innings at least per player was mandatory, and that was a requirement that I would need to uphold later as a coach myself. I played a little at second base but soon took on a more permanent role in the outfield. At one point, I played all three outfield positions, but because of my speed, I settled into center field. I also started to get more playing time there.

There was another reason that I was in the outfield. It was almost an unwritten law that your more experienced twelve-year-olds played in the infield, and the less experienced eleven-year-olds filled the gap in the outfield. After all, the ball has to go through the infield first before it gets to the outfield. Another law was that pitchers were usually the more experienced twelve-year-olds. We did have coaches who had the presence of mind to develop eleven-year-olds as future pitchers, whenever time and schedule permitted.

We also had the good fortune of having two seasoned pitchers in Dale Gestner and Lenny Harper. These two had remarkable speed and control for twelve-year-olds. Other pitchers in the rotation were Frank Reiss and eleven-year-olds John Parker and Bill Cook.

Looking back on this season, the thing that stands out in my mind the most was how we started to gel as a team. The Giants had a solid nucleus of talent and although we seemed to gravitate into assigned positions, the coaches were always willing to move players around and expand their baseball horizons. This team's cohesiveness was especially evident in practices, because although they were focused on improving our skills, they were also fun; it became common practice for the players to address each other as "brother": "brother Jim," "brother Bob," "brother Frank," and so on. It started to sound like a monastery.

It was in our first game against the Cardinals that I managed my first Little League hit. It was a fairly timid but meaningful swing that sent the ball past the second baseman and into right center field. As

I stood first base with my foot on the bag, it was a magic moment. I wasn't exactly an offensive threat my first year, only getting ten hits all season and batting .218. The hits and walks I did manage were timely and allowed me to develop another skill, which to this day I find one of the most exciting parts of the sport.

With the help of my speed and a streak of daring, I quickly became adept at base stealing. Now you need to know that in Little League, stealing bases is a special challenge because the rule states that you can't take a lead off a base or even start to run until the pitched ball reaches the batter. Since it's only a matter of a second between being by the batter and in the catcher's mitt, it doesn't leave much room for error. I had to start looking for ways to get around this obstacle.

One of my favorite techniques of baseball larceny involved watching the second baseman. Typically, the second baseman plays anywhere from ten to twelve feet to the right of the base, and the shortstop plays approximately the same distance, between second and third. I found that the key to stealing second base in Little League was not watching the pitcher or the catcher; it really involved watching these two guardians of second base. Since twelve-year-olds typically have the attention span of a cocker spaniel puppy, I would wait until just after the pitch, while the second baseman and shortstop were busy adjusting their belts or staring into their gloves for divine guidance. It would be then that I would take off like a shot out of a gun to second base. Yes, the catcher had the ball, but he had no one to throw it to. By the time these two protectors of second base realized what was happening, I was standing on the bag, dusting myself off. At a time when I was not exactly an offensive threat, it kept the game exciting and allowed me to contribute to the offense of the team. Just to add some spice to this strategy, I also had a variation where I would wait until the catcher caught the next pitch and was throwing it back to the pitcher. Just as he released the ball, I would take off for the next base. Again, by the time the pitcher received the ball and reacted to eight of his teammates screaming at him, I was standing on third base.

The bigger picture here is what I learned about what I was doing. The beauty of baseball is that there are so many ways in which you can help your team. You don't have to hit a home run every time up. This would prove to be a very valuable insight later on, especially coaching and counseling my sons and other kids in just about any sport.

I also learned to use my head on defense. We were playing the Braves one evening, and I was in center field. The Braves had a runner on second base; according to the rules, he had to wait until the pitch hit our catcher's glove, and then he would start dancing and jumping two or three feet off of second base. With each pitch, he would get a little farther off the base, but also with each pitch, I would take a few steps in from my center-field position until finally I was within five feet of the infield dirt behind second base. The runner was too busy with his antics to notice what was going on in back of him. Bobby, our catcher, realized what I was doing, and I could actually see the smile on his face right through the catcher's mask. After the next pitch was thrown, I darted the last five feet until I was practically standing on second base. Bobby caught the ball, the runner danced precariously off second base, and although the second baseman and shortstop never moved, Bobby gunned the ball down to second, into my waiting glove. The runner was out by two feet trying to get back.

Baseball seems to be a relatively simple game for people who don't understand it. As you begin to learn it, you realize that it is almost an athletic chess game. These types of plays and chances became more and more part of my playing style. The excitement that I generated for myself worked its way further into my performance and my attitude about coaching, subtly pushing the most timid player I ever coached into doing things they never thought they could do. What could be more fun?

As the season progressed, the Giants won on a regular basis, and we found ourselves in first or second place for most of the season. It seemed that everyone was getting better, and I was getting more aggressive at the plate. I was making more contact and felt more comfortable and confident at the plate and in the field. Finishing the season in first place would mean that we would represent our league in the citywide tournament in July. With one game to go, we had to play the Braves, who were in a flat-footed tie with us for first place. The night of that head-to-head matchup, I was as nervous as I was for the opening day exhibition. We knew it was going to be a close and hard-fought game; any mistake could decide the game.

I had seen it before. In a previous game with the Dodgers, we were tied going into the last inning. Mark Sanders, the Dodger ace, was pitching. We had managed to get two runners on but quickly had two outs. I was up with a semi poor record hitting against Mark. I'm sure he was reasonably certain he could get out of the inning with minimal damage. I managed to work out a count of two balls and two strikes, and then Mark came back with another fastball. I knew it was close and took a hard cut, just enough to tip the ball straight back on the screen. I guess Mark figured with a little more speed, he could end this. He let another pitch fly with a little too much energy, and it missed my left ear by just a few inches. Ball three, full count. Mark fired again and I managed another foul ball. The at-bat was taking longer than anyone anticipated. One more time, Mark came back with even more speed; the ball headed toward the outside part of the plate. It came in so fast I didn't have time to react and froze with the bat on my shoulder. I am not sure if the umpire just couldn't see the pitch or he felt sorry for me struggling to stay alive. He called, "Ball four."

The bases were loaded. I was on first, the winning run at third. Still, there was no need to panic. Alan Petrini was coming to the plate behind me. He was another rookie, with a slightly lower batting average than mine. Alan swung at the first pitch and missed it completely. This was going to be easy. Seeing the end in sight, Mark reared back and fired another pitch in toward home plate. As he did, he seemed to stumble on the pitching rubber. The ball sailed on Mark and was headed on a collision course with Alan. Poor Alan froze like a deer in the headlights, only with enough time to make a feeble hop so that his back was facing the pitcher. The ball hit him squarely in the buttocks as if it were a guided missile. At first everyone was frozen in time, not knowing whether to rush to Alan's aid or fall down on the field laughing. The brief silence was broken by the umpire's voice saying, "Take your base." Alan hobbled down to first, I trotted to second, the runner on second went to third, and the winning run crossed the plate in front of a horrified pitcher. We had won the game in a very unlikely fashion.

In the name of good sportsmanship, our league always required the winning team to go over to the losing dugout and congratulate the team on a game well played. We walked across the field and went down the line, shaking hands and mumbling "Nice game" about twelve times. It was probably eleven times, because Mark was tucked away in the back of the dugout with his glove over his face, sobbing uncontrollably. It was one of those times that confirmed for me that baseball can truly be a game of inches and that the distance between hero and goat in a game can be almost nothing.

The Showdown

So here we were, Giants and Braves, Braves versus Giants, mano-a-mano for the league championship and all the marbles. If we won the game, we were league champions and headed to the city tournament. If the Braves won, they needed only to beat the lowly Dodgers one more time and they were champions.

We had our best pitcher going, Dale Gestner, our ace, against Kenny Hill of the Braves. The game created a World Series atmosphere, and rookies and veterans were all on edge. We also had to sit through pregame team pictures, which prolonged the start of the game unmercifully. I remember sitting on the ground in the front row of the picture with a terrible case of butterflies, squinting into the late summer day sun. Looking back at that night, it has to be the worst picture of me ever taken.

The game wore on through three and four innings at a painfully close 1–1 score. Baseball has always been a game of inches, and single events can turn into major game breakers; this game would be no exception. Late in the fourth inning with a runner on, Bobbie Dickers, the Braves tall outfielder, caught a Dale Gestner fastball and hit it into the high screen that kept home-run balls from going out onto Asylum Street and possibly breaking a window at Giaquinto's Restaurant. My heart sank as I watched the ball head out of the park. This one swing of the bat seemed to close the door on what was otherwise a very successful and memorable first year in Little League. We did manage one more run but lost the game, 4–2.

There was a finality to this last game, as we put our bats back in the bag and received well wishes from the Braves. For the twelve-year-olds, I wasn't sure if I would ever play with them or even see them again. It would be the same empty feeling I would have at graduations and other milestones in my life.

It was a long ride home in the car that night. My mind raced ahead to consolation activities, since the Little League season seemed to be over. It was still early June; I still had our pickup games, Wiffle ball league, and a host of Yankee games to watch on television. I could still have a great summer, I thought.

Redemption

A few nights later, we were getting ready to have dinner when the phone rang. My mother answered and then handed the phone to me, announcing, "It's your coach." Coach Richards calmly explained, in his best Casey Stengel voice, that the Braves lost their very last game of the season to the lowly Dodgers. The last-place Dodgers, with nothing to lose, pounded the Braves 6–2, with Charlie Potts pitching his best game of the season. This unexpected loss knocked the first-place Braves back into a tie for first place with us. We had another date with destiny.

Because of the impending city tournament schedule, the game had to be completed before the end of the week. There would be no practice, the coach explained, just report to the field tomorrow night at 5:45 with a clean uniform and glove.

The next night, I arrived at the field at 5:30, ready to play. The same World Series atmosphere prevailed in this unexpected last night of baseball, but it was a bit more businesslike. There wasn't the same pregame pomp, no team picture session. Even the refreshment stand wasn't fully operational. Gum, candy, and french fries were the specials of the day. Hot dogs, hamburgers, and fried dough were packed away for the year.

Because of Little League rules for pitchers, neither team could start their number-one hurler. We started our next best pitcher, Lenny Harper. The Braves countered with their number two, Jim Riggs. Yes, Jimbo, one of my best friends and one of the few students in Thomas Hooker School with a better Rawlings Trapeze glove than mine.

The game was another nail biter, as expected, and moved along very methodically. There were two events that stood out in this game for me, even now, fifty years later. I was playing my typical spot in center field in the third inning when Jimbo came to the plate. I had enjoyed a reasonably good year playing center field, making some defensive plays that raised the eyebrows of my coaches a few times. My speed also helped me advance from playing the obligatory two innings, which most eleven-year-olds were destined for, to playing the whole game. Jim Riggs, one of my best friends, was the consummate twelve-year-old athlete; he was one of the best players in the league. He had already secured his spot on the All-Star team. He batted .509 for the season, which is incredible by any league's standards. He also was the second best pitcher on his team. About the only thing missing from his baseball credentials was a genuine over-the-fence home run.

Jimbo came to the plate in the third inning. Although a great hitter who usually hit the ball hard, he was a line drive hitter and usually didn't get the ball in the air. This was the main reason he didn't have a home run. Well, this at-bat was different. Jimbo launched a long fly ball to left center field, and I took off after it. This wasn't going to be your typical fly ball out, and I knew it. Now in the Major Leagues, they have a unique portion of real estate on the field called the warning track. When an outfielder is running for a fly ball, he is running on the grassy outfield. As he gets within a few feet of the fence, the grass changes to a dirt track, which, if he's running full speed and still paying attention, signifies to the outfielder that he is about to crash into the wall and break his nose. On a Little League field, there is no such track. My only saving grace was that I arrived at the outfield fence a second or two before the ball did, and as I ran into the fence, I groped for the top of it with my hand. I used the wall to launch myself and jumped as high as I could, and with my glove extended a foot or two over the fence, I felt the ball hit the pocket of my Trapeze glove.

On what turned out to be his last regular season at-bat of his Little League career, I had stolen the ultimate offensive prize from my friend and had preserved the lead for us in the game.

As though out of a Hollywood script, I was to bat second against Jimbo the next inning. As I stepped to the plate and rubbed dirt on my hands, I tried not to look directly into his face, which at that point was like peering into the sun. I never really saw his first pitch; I just heard it hit the catcher's glove. Seething with emotion, he had managed unprecedented speed but not much control. "Ball one!" barked the umpire. Two more similar attempts to take my head off met with the same results, and the count quickly went to three balls and no strikes.

Both the pitcher and the batter realized that the next pitch had to be a good one. Jimbo settled in and I, for the first time, looked him square in the eye. It looked for the entire world as though I was going to swing at this next pitch no matter what. As Jimbo reared back and kicked his leg to deliver the next pitch, I exaggerated a right leg lift as though I was going to take the swing of the century. As the pitch came in, I pulled back, holding my breath and letting the pitch go by. The ball sailed high and away, off the plate. "Ball four, take your base," ordered the umpire. I dropped the bat and trotted to first with my head down, just the way Mickey Mantle would have if he had hit one of his tape measure home runs.

A few pitches later, I stole second base, and after a few hits in back of me, I scored. We managed to push across another run in that inning and one more in the fifth. It wasn't a big lead, but Lenny was throwing with a vengeance that night, and the Braves only managed one run for themselves. As the sun began to set, Jimmy Walsh, the Braves catcher, grounded to Frank Reiss at third, who gunned the throw across to Norm Vance at first; game over. We were finally champions of Park City National Little League.

On to Black Rock

Black Rock Little League was host to the citywide Little League tournament in 1962. Teams all over the city, including our American League counterparts, the Park City American Indians, were slated to play a double elimination tournament. The winner would claim the title of city champions. The host team was the Black Rock Red Sox, and the tournament also included the East End White Sox and Bridgeport Originals, which proudly displayed the initials "BO" on their bright red baseball caps.

It was no accident that Black Rock was selected as the site for the tournament. The field was in even better shape than ours. It was also 200 feet down the right- and left-field lines and 210 feet to center.

It was a good 25 feet farther than our Park City Little League field. The fences that surrounded the field were not as high as ours, and my biggest fear was that if I had to repeat the circus catch I made against Jimbo in the playoffs, I might jump clear over the fence into the rock quarry below.

No one in this tournament was used to playing any of the other teams, so every game was an adventure. We had no clue how we stacked up to the competition. Our first game was with the East End White Sox. Dale pitched for us, and Kenny Henders pitched for East End. Ironically, East End was where I eventually spent my four high school years at Warren Harding High School. For now, East End Little League might as well have been in Texas.

The first game was on a hot day in late August, and our hosts went all out. It was truly a carnival-type atmosphere. The field was expertly manicured, and the white lines were actually a thick rubber stripe material that was fastened into place with small spikes. Odd but functional; I always love the look of the white limestone lines. A drum and bugle corps proudly opened the festivities and played the national anthem. Because of the number of games scheduled, there were friends and family streaming in and out all day. The refreshment stand was alive with the sights and smells of just about every picnic food you could think of. Even large pots of corn on the cob boiled just outside the door of the stand, away from the horseplay of smaller siblings. Corn on the cob . . . this was truly the big time!

There were a lot of strikeouts in this game. Both pitchers seemed to have saved their best performance for last. The game flew by, and before I knew it, we were on the wrong end of a 2–1 score. I didn't play the whole game, and there wasn't a lot of activity even when I was in the game. What was apparent was that we were already in a hole. If we repeated this performance one more time, we would be out of the tournament.

We entered the losers' bracket and played the host Black Rock Red Sox the very next day. This game turned out to be another close one and another day where we seemed to be flat. We couldn't really generate any offense; I struck out twice in this game to add to the two strikeouts I fell victim to in the first game. By the fourth inning, we were behind by a run, with no offense in sight. It looked as though our season would soon be over.

Allie Richards, our second baseman and Coach Richards's son, managed to draw a walk with one out. Lenny Harper, who had been pitching another gem, walked over to the bat rack, ready to take his turn. Lenny was our biggest player. He also was never known for mincing his words. After grabbing his bat like he was about to choke a chicken, he looked back at all the tired sweaty faces, including mine, and with a burst of frustration yelled, "I'm sick of this $%#*&!" He stormed out of the dugout and toward home plate.

Lenny let the first pitch go by, but the second pitch sounded like it was shot out of a gun. The ball took off toward straightaway center field: the worst possible place to hit a ball. At 210 feet out to the center field fence, it seemed like a mile. The ball never gained altitude, never sunk. It was like a laser beam. To this day, I can still see it go over the center field fence. I don't think I ever saw a ball hit that hard in a Little League game. Lenny ran the bases like he had atoned for a lifetime of sins.

After Lenny's home run, it was though we had a call to arms. We started to hit, run, and play defense as though we were possessed. We ended up winning the game and eliminating the host team. We went on to beat Bridgeport Originals, resulting in a rematch with the East End White Sox, who had beaten us in the very first game.

I continued to struggle at the plate, going hitless in eight trips to the plate. Even a hot dog and corn on the cob wasn't the answer. My parents used the two days off between the semifinal and final games to pitch Wiffle balls to me in the backyard. We tried to work on timing and hitting fastballs. It was really one of the first times in my relatively young sports career that I realized that these dry spells can be 80 percent mental and 20 percent physical. After a while you can talk yourself out of (or into) anything. We managed to get an early jump on the East End White Sox and never looked back, winning the game 4–1.

The Finale

Park City Little League had never won a city championship, but now one of our teams was sure to emerge victorious, because the two teams left standing for the final game were the Park City American Indians and my own Park City National Giants. We actually had a day to rest in between, which gave both teams a chance to start their best pitcher. Despite Lenny's pitching and hitting heroics, Dale was still our ace pitcher, and he got the nod on this day. Bobby Owens, who had been stellar for the Indians all year, was pitching for the Indians.

Before the last game, Coach Richards, our assistant coach, had been called up to the National Guard and would miss the game. Jim Worden, the vice president of the Park City Little League, stepped in as assistant coach. I personally didn't like the feel of this change. Coach Worden was a great guy, but I just didn't like the idea of this last-minute change. To me, it could only be a bad omen. Athletes can be a very superstitious lot. When a pro player is on a hot streak, he often refrains from shaving until the streak is broken. Substituting a coach at this point seemed to be the same as shaving in the middle of a streak for us.

It was a beautiful day in late August 1962 and, win or lose, this would be the last game of the season. I tried to put the last few games and my poor performance at the plate behind me.

I figured I would probably be back to an obligatory two innings and be designated as a first-base coach. After a few preliminaries and some warm-ups, we all gathered in the dugout for final words from the coaches. Coach Stott, with scorebook in hand, began to read off the starting lineup. "Batting first and playing center field, Jim C." My eyes widened. I was caught somewhere between joy and panic. I probably had the worst hitting performance on our team for the tournament. I was dumfounded that the coach was not only starting me but having me lead off! Had this man lost his mind? I walked over and grabbed my glove off the bench. I don't even remember hearing the rest of the lineup.

We were home team and, as such, took the field first. As I ran out of the third-base dugout, I repeated my superstitious act of always jumping over the chalk baseline so I wouldn't mess with its geometrical symmetry. It was bad luck. As I jumped over the white stripe, I remembered that it was just a rubber strip on this field and wondered if it even counted if I did step on it.

Dale must have had enough rest, because he was smoking hot in the first inning. He struck out two batters, and the third batter hit a weak ground ball that Frank Reiss scooped up and turned into an easy out. I made my way into the dugout and headed right to the bat rack. I picked out a batting helmet and had a quick flash back to the second game with the East End White Sox. In the fourth inning of that game, I managed to get on base after the pitcher lost control of a fastball. As I tried to duck instinctively away from the pitch, I turned toward the pitcher and the ball hit me square in the helmet. The helmet cracked right down the middle from the top to the ear holes, like a fresh egg. My ears were ringing, but I was awarded a trip to first base.

I smiled as I put on the helmet and picked out my bat. Standing next to the catcher, watching Bobby O take his last warm-ups, I decided to put past history behind me. I stepped into the batter's box and heard the umpire snap, "Play ball!"

It was a warm summer morning, and the sun was at my back. It made the brand-new ball look even whiter and brighter than normal. I thought back to the pickup games we had in the schoolyard with the beat-up ball covered with black electrical tape. This truly was the Show.

Bobby's first pitch came in about letter-high and on the outside corner of the plate. I never hesitated; I was going to get this over with. I could feel the vibes of good luck coming from my parents in the stands. I took my best cut at the pitch and heard an unfamiliar crack. I looked up to see that brand-new white baseball bouncing gingerly through the infield, just between the second baseman and first baseman. It was a clean hit to right field, and I had started our rally. After a fielder's choice and another hit, we had managed to push one run across the plate. It was a good start but there was a lot of baseball yet to be played.

The run in the first inning turned out to be very valuable because for the next five innings there was nothing. No runs for either side. Bobby O and Dale were in a pitchers' strikeout duel for the ages. Only a few meaningless hits were scattered throughout the game. It was now the top of the sixth. Dale was on the mound and still looking great. Three more outs and it would be over. I was still in the game in the sixth inning, and still wondering why, but I vowed to make the most of my opportunity. As the morning wore on, the early morning clouds gave way to a cloudless blue sky. It was great for postcards, but as an outfielder, I hated it. When there are no clouds, you have no depth perception on a ball that is hit in the air.

Dale struck out the first batter in the sixth, and then Kenny James came to the plate. He was the tallest player on the Indians and one of the best hitters. He was also the only black player in the entire Park City Little League; come to think of it, he was one of the players I ended up playing tag with in the basement of St. Charles Church during opening day Mass. Talk about coming full circle!

Apparently Kenny thought it was time for a change, and he caught one of Dale's fastballs and sent it high in the air to—yes, you guessed it—left centerfield. I was off with the crack of the bat, looking frantically up at the cloudless sky. There it was! I had a bead on it, and it looked as though it was going to stay in the park. The ball seemed to be bouncing wildly in the sky, and I was really having trouble picking it up. A little voice reminded me in the last few steps to run on my toes and not my heels. It greatly reduces that bouncing effect. I caught up with the ball and felt it hit my glove. The emergency and panic was over for now. Two outs.

Flash Forward

Years later, I would meet Mickey Mantle in LaGuardia Airport, boarding a flight for Dallas. We actually boarded side by side, and I had an opportunity to talk to him for a few minutes. Of the two thousand questions I wanted to ask him, the one I was able to get out was, "When were you the most nervous on the field?"

Mickey smiled and said, "The last inning of Don Larsen's perfect game against the Brooklyn Dodgers in the 1956 World Series. All I kept saying to myself was, please don't let them hit it to me." This thought came just a few innings after Mantle made what he considered the best catch of his career off a long fly ball hit by Gil Hodges. That incredible catch preserved the perfect game at that point.

That is exactly where my head was with this last batter. Two outs, last inning, 1–0 Giants: "Please don't let them hit it to me." Dale knew he was down to his last three or four pitches for the year, which meant he wasn't holding anything back. The batter worked the count to two balls and two strikes. I was holding my breath with every pitch. The next pitch was right down the middle with all the smoke Dale had left. The batter didn't come close with his swing. "Strike three!" Game over! Point, set, match! City champs! We all raced to the pitcher's mound in a wild mass of bodies, caps thrown in the air like a West Point graduation.

From time to time, I reflect on this season. Even as an adult, I read between the lines of baseball and find a greater treasure. I took much away from the 1962 season for myself, my family, my boys, and the many young people I would coach in the future. Yogi Berra, the great Yankee catcher, once said, "It ain't over till it's over." I think back about our loss to the Braves, which almost dethroned us from our league championship and kept us out of the city tournament. Winning the tournament was even less likely, but we did it. I thought about having our backs against the wall in the game against Black Rock, and how with sheer will and determination Lenny turned the entire tournament around for us with one swing of the bat. I also think about the terrible hitting slump I found myself in, and the frustration of not being able to contribute as much as I wanted to. The fact was, for me, that I only had one hit in the entire tournament, but that one hit led to the only run in the final game.

Yes, this season unknowingly helped me through some of the toughest periods of my life and also allowed me to provide support and confidence to future generations of sports fans and athletes. I left Black Rock Field feeling very proud that I could be part of such a team accomplishment. I began to think about what next year would bring and wondered if it was too early in the morning for corn on the cob.

The Giants of 1963: I'm a Veteran

I was in seventh grade, twelve years old, when I started my second year in Little League. I was still a year away from graduating eighth grade and moving on to a new school. It was still a year before I would experience leaving some friends for the first time and moving on to new ones. Our first practice of the 1963 season brought some of those changes for the first time. We did have some returning eleven-year-olds from last year, including John P., Johnny V., Alan P., and Billy Cook. We also had a new contingent of eleven-year-old rookies, who would make up a remarkably different brotherhood than we had last year.

I watched the first practice unfold and took special note of how both coaches assessed the new talent, deciding what holes needed to be filled. I was somewhat surprised but flattered that the coaches decided to position me at shortstop. Typically you put your best two players at shortstop and first base. I didn't really have time to get settled, however, because I started moving around. A truly unexpected change in position for me occurred two games before opening day. Coach Richards had me put on the catcher's gear: mask, shin pads, chest protector, the whole works. I was a little surprised at the choice of position for me since I was always considered one of the fastest of my school peers at the time. There is no more confining position on the field than catcher.

I wasn't sure if I was that good as a catcher or there was no one else on the team that wanted the dirty, demanding, thankless job. As we moved closer to opening day, it looked as though I was going to land the catcher's job. What sealed the deal was that in the last practice before opening day, I was given the "cup." This triangular plastic and foam rubber insert fit awkwardly in an elastic waistband that you wore inside your uniform pants. Strategically placed, the cup fit over your most vulnerable area as a twelve-year-old boy, in case the catcher's gear wasn't sufficient.

Opening day finally arrived, and the first thing I noticed was that there wasn't the same festival atmosphere as there was the previous season. There was no Mass, no breakfast, and no parade. All I wanted to do was play ball, so it didn't matter to me at the time, but I realize now that it is hard work to orchestrate that type of fanfare. The same dedicated adults take on those challenges every year, and it becomes a given that these people will be around forever. If no one else steps up, things can slip. I didn't see it clearly as a twelve-year-old but became very familiar with this truth as an adult and coach.

We all arrived at the field on opening day; we were scheduled to play the Cardinals, the team that my best friend Billy played on. After assembling in the dugout and going through the preliminary ceremonies, I sat on the bench and subtly adjusted my cup through my uniform. In one of life's most ironic moments, Coach Richards looked down the bench at me and said, "Jim C, go warm up." I grabbed the catcher's mitt, assuming he wanted me to warm up the starting pitcher. "No, no," Coach Richards snapped, "you're pitching. Go warm up with Johnny V." I was going to pitch in my first Little League game, and I was going to do it against my best friend's team.

I finished my warm-up pitches and walked back into the dugout with the catcher just in time to hear the reading of the lineup. It was true. I was not only pitching, I was batting cleanup, or fourth in the lineup, usually reserved for the best hitter on the team. I didn't have time to think about it though because we were home team, which meant we had to take the field first.

I walked to the freshly manicured pitcher's mound and looked at the white rubber with a fresh white rosin bag placed to the side of the rubber. Now, rosin is used to dry the pitcher's sweaty hands during the game, but it probably isn't really necessary for Little Leaguers. However, the rosin bag was on the pitcher's mound of every Major League game ever played, so that was enough for me.

I picked up the brand-new ball and threw a few practice pitches, trying not to look into the Cardinal dugout. It was too late. I could hear Billy laugh in disbelief. It didn't help my ego to hear him telling the rest of his team, "He's no pitcher. We can hit him."

I managed three innings and didn't allow any runs, although I ran into a little trouble in the third inning. I didn't realize at the time but my pitching mechanics left much to be desired, so much so that the ball usually came out of my hand slower that it looked like it should have. That became my saving grace for most of the year. Joe Hansen, the cleanup hitter for the Cardinals, struck out swinging on a pitch that I tried to throw as hard as I could, but the pitch arrived deceptively slower than it looked. He missed this optical illusion completely with his mighty swing.

Billy Cook came on in relief in the fourth inning, and I was never so disappointed and happy at the same time. I did manage to get two hits in the game. We won the game, 4–1, and we were off and running again.

The season moved on pretty rapidly. I was off to a great start, enjoying at least two hits every game and settling into a leadership role at shortstop. I was, through no fault of my own, relegated to the third pitcher in the rotation behind John and Billy Cook. That was fine with me. It was just enough. Objectively speaking, pitching was just one of nine positions on the field. I did learn that what Billy and I always talked about was special. Pitching was special. When you were on the mound, you were geometrically in the middle of the entire game. You were also on your own. You had the ball almost every play. The fortunes of the game would rise and fall to a great extent on your ability to keep the batters off balance and to stifle their efforts to score runs. I will never forget the feeling of being on the pitcher's mound. It was the coach's way, and the team's way, of saying, "We trust you enough to place our confidence and fate in your hands. You may rise to victory or stumble in defeat, but we are with you, and we will go where you go."

Paying It Forward

Thirty years later, I would remember this feeling and use it as a coach. Sharing that same feeling was important to me. I wanted another young baseball player to feel the same rush of pride. I wanted once again to feel the chills that go up your back. When I was coaching Jim Jr.'s Little League team, we had our share of skilled eleven- and twelve-year-olds, and some that were, well, let's say never going to be Major Leaguers. One of those players was Kevin, one of the smaller boys on the team, even for eleven. Kevin played right field, because no one usually hits to right field. He did have perfect attendance at practice and was present for every game. You could never fault his attitude or enthusiasm. Kevin would come up to me at one point in just about every practice and, with all the courage he could muster, inquire, "Coach, do you think I might be able to pitch sometime?" I could feel his pain at my negative answer, but realistically, we had a complete pitching staff, and I had also experimented with some other promising eleven-year-olds. This never stopped Kevin from persistently and politely asking if he could pitch. His father also interceded at one point on his behalf, and I explained the situation, not wanting to make a promise I couldn't keep.

One Saturday morning before practice, I was going over the day's agenda with my wife, Beth. One of those agenda items on the "to do" list was practice. At one point, in the middle of the conversation on practice and what to do about Kevin, Beth simply quipped, "Why don't you let him pitch a little in practice? What is it going to hurt? Are the baseball police going to come and arrest you?" What a revelation! She was absolutely right! If I positioned it properly, there was no downside to this. Leave it to her to defy all logic and cut to the heart of the matter.

During hitting practice, as I was moving players around the field, I casually asked Kevin if he would pitch to a few batters. Kevin looked at me as though I had instantly grown another head, and before I could finish the sentence, he was standing on the pitcher's mound. He actually didn't pitch too badly once he loosened up and stopped throwing the ball over the catcher's head. This little exercise of having Kevin throw batting practice was repeated selectively throughout the rest of the season. At the time, Kevin and I both knew that this was as close to pitching as he was realistically going to get.

During the next-to-the-last game of the season, our team had one of those nights where we couldn't do anything wrong. We had built up a 13–2 lead going into the last inning. Jim Jr. had personally pounded the opposition with three hits and three RBIs. I decided to bring in one of our promising eleven-year-olds to pitch the fourth and fifth inning, and we were still able to maintain a sizable lead.

As we began the last inning, I was standing on the stairs of the dugout with one eye on the game and the other in the scorebook I was holding. Last inning, three outs to go. Crack of the bat, ground ball to second, over to first, one out! The next batter stepped in. I looked out, surveying the field, and saw Kevin in right field, waving. I followed his gaze and saw his parents standing by the fence down the right-field line. All of sudden I got an idea that made me smile to myself.

Calling timeout, I walked out to the mound and complimented our pitcher on his performance, adding that I wanted to make a quick change. I looked into right field, and Jeff rolled his eyes but smiled and understood. I waved out to right field, motioning to Kevin to come in. At first he stood motionless as though I were beckoning to someone else, everyone else besides him, but finally he realized what I was asking.

Kevin probably set a land speed record coming in from right field to the pitcher's mound, where he met me, huffing, puffing, and grinning, his eyes wide through his thick glasses. "Kevin," I said, "finish this game up for us . . . relax and have fun."

Kevin eagerly took some quick warm-up pitches, and just before the hitter stepped in, he stole a look over at his parents, who had moved much closer down the fence to just in back of first base. I could never capture in words the look that passed between Kevin and his parents. I do know that for a moment, Kevin and I were both one. That was me again, thirty years earlier, standing on that field during the first game of the 1963 season. The first time I stood on that mound, toed that bright white rubber, and stared down at the catcher's mitt on a warm summer evening. Kevin gave up a walk and a hit, but he got us through the inning, and we all headed to the bleachers for our victory round of hot dogs and sodas. This was a tradition I inherited from my coaches. Players were eating, parents and siblings were milling around, and I looked over at Kevin. He was looking at me, glasses a little crooked on his nose and some mustard on the corner of his mouth. He just smiled a smile I will never forget. It was a smile that only he and I could appreciate at that moment. It was a smile of a sacred bond, a shared experience that was separated by thirty years. My hope was that when my thirty years turned into his thirty years, he would find a way to pass that feeling forward.

Practice Makes Perfect

I thought it was ironic that our team, the Giants, had the most success of any of the teams in our league over the 1962 and '63 seasons. It was ironic because we also had the worst practice field of any team in the league. While the rest of the league conducted regularly scheduled practices on the well-manicured fields of Beardsley Park, the Giants were relegated to the confines of Glenwood Park. I was never really sure what this park was for. It had one abandoned baseball diamond with a broken and rotting wooden backstop. The base paths were overgrown with more than its share of rocks and uneven ground. It had one aging picnic table that you would think twice about placing any food on. Finally, there was a stream that ran inconveniently along the third-base line; we regularly had to wade through water up to our knees retrieving batted and thrown balls.

To this day, I have to credit this eyesore at least in part to our team's success. The rough field turned even the simplest infield ground ball drill into a pinball machine of erratic movement. If you didn't keep your eye on the ball constantly, you could lose it at any time. Along with that physical degree of difficulty, our coach pitched constant batting practice, seeming to forget that we were eleven and twelve years old. Coach Stott would pitch with the force and speed that high school players would find challenging. The amazing thing is that we all learned to hit him and hit him well. Once you could hit Coach Stott, you could hit anyone.

Our coaches found ways to make practice fun but educational and with the discipline that says to treat practice like you would a game. If you goofed off and practiced without discipline, you can bet you will do the same in a game. "You play like you practice" was a valuable lesson for me. The most significant difference between sports and life is that in just about any sport, you can call timeout and stop the clock . . . even if only for a few moments. In life, there are no timeouts. The clock is always running. Looking back on both seasons, I can't ever remember missing a practice.

The Last Days as a Giant

By midseason, I was hitting the ball very well. My parents provided me with some added incentive to hit well by offering a Dairy Queen ice cream sundae for every hit I got. As a rookie, I had nine hits. I finished the 1963 season with thirty-two hits. I can't say that the promise of ice cream had all that much to do with it, but it was a great gesture. I was seeing the ball well and hitting the ball all over the park. My swing improved to where I was really a line drive hitter. I very seldom hit a fly ball anywhere.

The downside of that was the elusive hit-the-ball-over-the-fence, out-of-the-park, trot-around-the-bases home run. One night against the Braves, I hit a hard line drive to right center field. I put my head down and started running hard to first base. I looked up briefly to see the ball disappear over the fence. I couldn't believe it. I had finally hit one out. As I victoriously jogged around second base and headed toward third in my celebratory trip, the umpire's voice brought me back to earth. "Second base, son," he said. It seemed that the ball had bounced over the fence, and in any rule book that becomes a ground rule double. The dream would have to wait.

What made the over-the-fence home run even more precious was punctuated by a game soon after. It was not uncommon for Billy and me to attend each other's games when we weren't playing. One night, I was watching his Cardinals play the Dodgers. It was the fourth inning and Billy was up. I was enjoying the view from just over the left field fence, munching on my hot dog. Suddenly there was a crack of the bat, and I looked up to see a fly ball off Billy's bat headed in my direction. It kept coming and eventually hit the screen a few feet away from me, having cleared the fence. It was a genuine, over-the-fence home run! Little Leaguers typically get to keep their home-run ball, and this event was no exception. That night during the ride home, Billy caressed that ball like it was the Hope diamond. It was interesting because two good friends got to share rare and different trophies of Little League. He had hit a genuine over-the-fence home run, and I had the chance to pitch in a game. Neither of us ever had the chance to experience the other's sacred prize. I guess it is one of the things that make life unpredictable and interesting.

As a veteran, I still was not immune from my share of mistakes. One night, we were in the middle of a rally, and I came to bat with the bases loaded. As I stepped into the batter's box, Coach Richards yelled for my attention and then fired off a flurry of signals to me. It was then that I realized that I had forgotten the pregame signals we were given. Not one to panic, I tried to use logic. I was obviously in a hitting situation with the bases loaded, so what signal would he give me? He wouldn't want me to take a pitch, let it go by, because I was one of the best hitters on the team. The only thing left was the bunt! *I am not sure why, but that must be it,* I thought. I nodded and stepped back into the batter's box. The first pitch came right down the middle, and I squared my shoulders and dropped a perfect bunt down the first-base line.

The infielders, along with our bench and my coaches, looked at the slowly rolling ball as though it was a flying saucer that just landed on the field. "No!" screamed Coach Richards. When the infielders came out of their temporary state of shock, the first baseman made a mad dash for the ball. Realizing there was no play at home plate, he quickly wheeled and threw the ball to third base. The ball sailed four feet over the third baseman's head, hitting the fence and bounding erratically into left field.

When the dust cleared, three runs had scored and I was on second base. I had three runs batted in on a ball that traveled about thirty feet. Even as far away as second base, I could hear Coach Stott consoling Coach Richards as he sat with his Giants cap over his face.

Defensively, I look back and realize that in the course of my two years in Little League, I had played every position on the field during the game. I know that the coaches attempted to make me a more complete player and at the same time gave the same experiences to my teammates. I even played the lackluster position of right field.

One night, while we were playing the last-place Dodgers, I was moved over to right field to back up the rookie who was getting his first chance to play second base. In the fourth inning, Denny Bates came up to the plate for the Dodgers. Denny was a great kid, with a huge sense of humor and a body to match. As a twelve-year-old, Denny must have weighed 225 pounds if he weighed an ounce. Because of his size and lack of mobility, he was the Dodger catcher. He also managed to go one-and-three-quarter seasons without getting one hit. His average stood at .000. Denny stood at the plate, and just about the time I was wishing I had a lawn chair, he swung at a fastball and ripped it to right field. The ball took one hard bounce in front of me and landed right in my glove. I didn't even have to move.

Now, according to basic baseball strategy, when a batter hits a single, the outfielder throws the ball into second base (or to the cutoff man who is close to second base). This prevents the runner from turning a single into a double. As I fielded the ball and began my throw to second base, I instinctively looked up and saw Denny, barely out of the batter's box, lumbering down the line like a water buffalo trying to escape a charging lion. I'm not sure if it was my baseball instincts or the devil that pushed me into what happened next. Realizing that Denny wasn't going to be getting to first base anytime soon, I gunned a perfect strike to Norm Vance, our first baseman. As I let the ball go, I realized what I had done and wished I could have had it back. Denny was out by four feet. His one chance at a hit in a Little League game was gone.

Well, God eventually forgave me and smiled on Denny in the very next game. Denny did get his first hit. The more significant realization for me was that I was really starting to understand the game and create opportunities where there were none. I began to understand when the opposition made a mistake and how to capitalize on it.

During our next game with the Cardinals, I cracked a clean double and pulled up at second base. As I did, I saw that the third baseman had drifted down the third-base line until he was only about six feet from home plate. Yes, that's right, there was absolutely no one covering third base! Again, without really thinking, I took off for third. By the time the pitcher, catcher, and third baseman realized the mistake, I was already standing on third base.

Later in that same game, I finally captured my elusive home run. I came up to bat against Kenny Fender. Kenny's second pitch was letter-high and just slightly inside. I turned on it and hit a hard line drive right down the left-field line. It stayed in the air longer than it should have and finally bounced only three feet from the fence. As it hit the fence, it took an unexpected kick off the wooden advertisement board and started to run along the fence toward center field. Because of my speed, I was almost at second base when the ball hit the fence. I kept going and looked to the third-base coach, his arms now waving like a windmill in a hurricane. "Go home! Go home!" he screamed. Home I went, sliding into the plate when I didn't have to. A legitimate home run, even if it never left the park.

Every game that year seemed to be a precious chapter of great baseball memories, a chance to bond with my school friends and enjoy an occasional hot dog after the game. It was even more fun because my Giants were again at the top of the league standings.

The season came down to the last game between my Giants and the Braves, and once again we were tied for first place. The winner of the game would be league champs for 1963. It was the usual back-and-forth game that you would expect from two first-place contenders. The Braves managed a two-run lead going into the last inning, but our spirits were high, knowing we had the best hitters coming up in the bottom of the sixth. We managed to string a few hits together and score a run, but we came up just short and lost by just a single run.

I remember only two things that happened immediately after. Even though we lost, we still received a celebratory hot dog and soda for a great year. The other was that I sat in the backseat of my father's car, next to my friend Billy, on the way home, and I was sobbing. I was sobbing because for all intents and purposes, my Little League experience was over. I had a memorable two years, about thirty games, give or take, and enjoyed some incredible experiences playing the game I loved more than anything. I was going to find out shortly that the end of the season had not yet occurred; there was more to come.

Park City Little League All Stars

I said previously that there were two very coveted events that we all wished for in our Little League experience. One was to actually pitch in a game, to be the pitcher standing on the mound as the center of attention. The second was to hit a home run. A real over-the-fence, trot-around-the-bases home run. Well, there was actually a third coveted event.

The third goal was to make the Little League All-Star team. Now there were four teams in each league, with twelve players on the roster, so roughly fifty players in the American and fifty in the National league. The All-Star team was a roster of the twelve best players in each league. Selection was not exactly a national honor but a great accomplishment by anyone's standards.

After the disappointing season-ending loss to the Braves, my family packed the car and left for a summer week in Wilkes-Barre, Pennsylvania, to visit my grandmother, aunts, and cousins. Yes, we had Wiffle ball pickup games there too, and they even had an ice cream man.

In the summer of 1963, there wasn't a lot going on back home; according to Billy's mother, he sat around and kicked at the dirt the week I was gone, waiting for me to return. I don't think we had all the suitcases unpacked from the trip when our phone rang. It was Billy. "Glad you're back," he said, "and oh, you made the All Stars." Sure enough, a day later my phone rang and it was Mr. Munson, the All-Star coach, giving me the official news and telling me when practice was scheduled. Coach Munson was the All-Star coach as a result of his Braves winning the league championship. Ah, life can be so cruel!

The most notable thing about the All Stars was getting the cap. It was a special cap with "PCLL" on it and two honest-to-goodness stars on either side. There were only six boys in my seventh-grade class with Little League team hats, out of a class of thirty. There were only two with All-Star hats, and I was one of them!

As far as the All-Star experience itself, it was relatively short and uneventful. We had a few practices at our home field. You could tell it was postseason because during one practice, a ball was hit into the outfield that I literally lost in the six-inch-high grass.

The tournament was even more unmentionable. We only lasted one game and were eliminated by the Westport National All Stars, 5–2. I only played two innings in right field and never got to bat. The game was played at the same Black Rock field where we won the city championship the previous year. If there was an irony to all this, it was that there would be no city tournament that year. The Stratford All Stars made it all the way to Williamsport, Pennsylvania, that year to play in the Little League World Series. Because of that amazing feat, every Little League official was either preparing for that trip or going on it. There was no city tournament and no city champ. I suppose I had some comfort in knowing that the Braves championship was a hollow one at best. They never played one more game than we did after that night. The blessing in disguise here is that All Stars could have easily been the first real sports commitment I would have had to make. Those teams that had gone on well into the tournament had their all-too-precious summer completely engulfed in practices, games, and trips, most of them out of state.

Later as an adult, I would read about young athletes who gave up their summers (and in some cases, their childhoods) in the name of athletic excellence.

It's Not All about Baseball

Little League baseball was an opportunity to play my favorite sport at the highest level or competition and under the most authentic conditions you could imagine, right down to uniforms, white chalked lines, and fans in the stands. With that came a certain pride, a pride that seems to be missing, and one that I hope young people can somehow experience the way I did.

We were not just Little League baseball players. We did, to a great extent, own the entire experience. For example, every few weeks during the season, the league would schedule two teams to take part in "Field Day." We spent a Saturday at the field in work clothes, helping to cut the grass, empty the trash, clean out the refreshment stand, paint, or repair as necessary. Did you ever paint a fence with a roller full of silver paint? Take it from me, you need to wear old clothes.

At the beginning and the end of every game, two or three of us would be picked to go down the right-field line and grab the old, heavy rug that was stored there. We would drag the rug around the infield, erasing cleat marks, stones, and other obstacles and make the infield smooth as a pool table. When you ran the new white-chalked foul lines, I swear it looked like Yankee Stadium. You wanted to play on a field like that.

Fast Forward

A few years ago, I went back to the same field where we dragged that carpet around the infield. It was the same field where I painted the fence and the same one that I spent opening day, standing at attention while the national anthem blared through the public address system. There was grass and weeds growing in the infield. The fences surrounding the field were bent and rusty. Some of the bleachers were broken or missing, and the beloved refreshment stand was boarded up. I wanted to believe that after almost fifty years, life had moved on and that the league found a better place to play: a new field, new press box, and refreshment stand. I left my car on the street and walked through the same gate that our opening day parade passed through during that memorable summer of 1962. I walked by the same dugout that Mark Sanders sat in, sobbing over his heartbreaking last-minute loss. I stood at home plate, looking out into the weed-infested infield, where I had stood so many times before.

I felt that I was standing in a graveyard, a cemetery of what used to be, and I realized you can never go home again. I was content to rationalize what I was seeing as just that. I walked back though the rusty broken gate that separated the field from the bleachers. As I walked slowly toward the street and my car, I heard young voices. I looked up to see three or four boys and an adult walking toward me. The boys were dressed in blue T-shirts that said "Giants." They wore jeans or shorts with no attempt to match a standard uniform. They were carrying gloves, and the older man was carrying the familiar coach's bag. I realized there was a game tonight.

I wondered why such hallowed ground for me had made such a downturn. If I could blame it on the failing economy, placing youth recreational activities in a "nice to have," not a "need to have," category, I could understand it. If I could rationalize the change that now many parents are working two jobs and have precious little discretionary time, I could bite my lip and nod in agreement. My biggest fear and disappointment was that apathy and indifference had settled in with both parents and children. Video games, big-screen TVs, and many other competing activities were snuffing the life out of a place I had so treasured.

Little League Keepsake

Each year at the conclusion of our Little League schedule, we would have the annual Little League banquet. Players, teammates, family, and friends would gather at Mary Journey's Inn on Black Rock Turnpike for chicken parmesan, spaghetti, speeches, and awards. We usually had a guest speaker from the Major Leagues (not a big star) to do a short speech toward the end of the banquet, right before the presentation of awards.

The banquet was another facet of the sporting experience that a twelve-year-old would take for granted. When I think now of the timing and planning it must have taken to schedule it, arrange it, invite everyone, order food, print tickets, negotiate a speaker, and get dozens of trophies bought and engraved, it makes my head spin. As a player, I must say it was worth it. Chicken and a trophy was a great finishing touch to an experience that started on spring Saturday morning with Mass, a breakfast, and a parade.

After my second and last year as a Little Leaguer, I got another special keepsake. Graduating twelve-year-olds were issued a Little League jacket. It was a black felt winter jacket. It had light beige leather sleeves and a bright orange Little League patch on the left breast pocket. As a league All Star, I additionally had the All-Star pin affixed conspicuously to the Little League patch. Wearing that jacket to school, and sometimes to bed, was quite a statement that you were part of an elite group. I can picture that jacket even now with a smile. It was the absolute cherry on my Little League sundae.

Football (Not the Soccer Kind) at the Park

Most of my personal sports experience to this point had been in baseball, for a very good reason. Baseball was really the sport that was most promoted, most televised, and most readily available as a local organized sport. Professional basketball games were few and far between, usually televised at night. Football was the number-two sport, and because it was seasonal we usually played some type of football from mid-October after the World Series, to somewhere around February or March.

Football, like a good classical musical symphony, had some variation on a theme. There was tackle football, played with or without equipment: pads, helmets, and so on. There was also touch football, which could be further divided into one-hand or two-hand touch.

Finally, there was flag football, not as rough and knockdown as tackle football, but more decisive than touch football. Each player wore two strips of cloth in his belt on either side. The object was to pull the strip of cloth out of the belt of the ball carrier to stop the play. This act was in lieu of touching him with one or two hands or tackling him to the ground. As exciting as that might sound, the preferred version was tackle football with equipment.

Most days after school we played pickup football at Beardsley Park. Earlier, I expounded on the necessity of us all being organized and efficient in order to pull off a game in a relatively small amount of time. Let me briefly review this impossible schedule for you.

After-School Football Schedule

3:15 p.m.	Dismissal from school
3:30 p.m.	Home to change, grab helmet, shoulder pads, and bike
3:50 p.m.	Bike ride and arrival at Beardsley Park
3:50 to 4:00 p.m.	Pick sides, set up field
4:00 to 5:00 p.m.	Game time
5:00 to 5:15 p.m.	Bike ride home
5:15 p.m.	What's for dinner?

This whole experience took two hours at the most. What made the schedule even more pressing was that in the waning days of fall, the days began to get shorter, to the point where the last fifteen minutes of the game, it was starting to get dark.

We usually managed to recruit anywhere from eight to twelve regulars for our games. It was a random ragtag group of different colored helmets and jerseys or sweatshirts that covered shoulder pads. We all wore old sneakers because mud and rain were sometimes an extra challenge. On sunny autumn days, the sky was a solid blue and the fall leaves exploded in reds and yellows in contrast. You could smell the remnants of the last mowed grass of the year along with the scent of hay and leaves that had already fallen. The solid blue sky was not a problem because there were no fly balls.

These pickup games were a precursor to formal teams that we assembled to play other schools. Our team only consisted of six players. Four of these players were in the backfield, with a two-man line. Looking back, I am not sure what we intended to do with that type of organizational chart. We did practice almost daily during our eighth-grade lunch hour at school. Our quarterback was Jim Riggs (Jimbo). Billy and I were the halfbacks, Paul Clark was the center, and John Blare was an end. Jimbo lived right across the street from the school, and we would carry a miniature football around and could assemble very quickly to execute a practice with almost no notice.

Out team had an interesting array of creative offensive plays. They included "Right and Left Half Cross Buck," alternate plays with a fake to one halfback while handing off to the other as they crossed in front of the quarterback, and "Twenty-Five Fly," a deep crossing pass pattern. The favorite, however, was a play called "Bushes." This play was named for the hedges that encircled Jimbo's front yard and our practice field. As innocent as "Bushes" sounds, it was a formidable, nasty play. It consisted of a very quick count and snap. Once Jimbo had the ball, he would quickly fire the ball with all his earthly might at me. I was positioned about ten feet to the left of the center on the line. I would catch the pass, mostly out of self-defense, and take off down field with my unmatched speed. Because it happened so quickly, it was almost always a sure touchdown—providing the ball didn't hit me in the head and knock me cold! I have no proof, but I suspect that Jimbo devised this play solely to get back at me for catching his home-run ball during the last Braves-Giants playoff game.

Although we were disciplined in our practices, the logistics of finding another team with that configuration became too hard. The practices were fun and satisfied the need to emulate our favorite football stars that we watched every Sunday.

Basketball: The Third Sport

I never felt the need to fill every day of the calendar year with sports activities. I didn't necessarily have a sport for every season. Baseball lasted from April to the World Series, which promptly ended the first week in October. By then, college and pro football were on weekend television, and I could catch a game or two if I was not busy with other activities. We loved being out in the snow, building forts and snowmen, having massive snowball fights. We also had winter Cub Scout meetings indoors.

It wasn't until we started playing indoor winter games as part of recess in the fourth and fifth grade that I was introduced to the game of basketball. At first it was just part of a coed fourth-grade relay in the gym. Gradually that relay tuned into an abbreviated half-court version of a real basketball game. I had a feeling that no one in our school faculty was really knowledgeable about the game, and as rules go, it was usually left to an informal shooting spree.

Back to the Driveway (Basketball Initiation)

My real initiation to basketball came when my father bought and then installed my very own basket and backboard on our garage. He did a great job installing it, and only now do I realize that it must have been a difficult challenge to position it on the face of the garage and fasten it securely without any help. With a brand-new basketball to go with it, I was able to come right home from school, change clothes, and be out in the driveway shooting in no time.

The thing about basketball is that it is definitely a team sport. Shooting by yourself in the driveway is just scratching the surface. About the time I started to realize that, the neighborhood kids started to notice the basket hanging on the garage. Occasionally I would be out shooting, sometimes with my father, when the usual suspects—Billy, Jimbo, and John Blare—would appear, and before long, sides were picked and a game started.

As these games became more frequent, more organized, and more populated, I realized a few things. One was that there was a lot more to the game than just shooting the ball. The other revelation was that I really didn't have a clear idea of what those other things were that I was supposed to do.

The games got to a point where we had four or five on a side, which was too much for a one-car driveway and garage basketball court. I was demoted from host to one step above a spectator, positioning myself in a stationary spot on the corner of the driveway. If a pass from a teammate happened to come to me, I would make every attempt to get a shot off before I was descended upon by multiple flailing arms and legs.

These games were played after school, usually in that dead space between the end of football season and March, when we could start breaking out the baseball gloves. That meant that most of these games involved the pregame preparation of shoveling off the driveway and chipping ice so that we all didn't wind up in the hospital. Even when there was no snow, the ground was usually soaking wet and very muddy. You could never really dribble or shoot a basketball with any type of gloves, so the gloves came off. If the temperature outside was freezing or below, you could hardly feel your hands after the first ten minutes of the game. Having a wet, muddy, or snowcapped ball made shooting even more challenging, and your hands started looking like you just replaced the engine of a Ford F-150.

Since there never seemed to be any formal instruction or coaching around for basketball, I looked at it as the free-for-all that it seemed to be. I was always glad when baseball season started to come around.

Hooker's Seventh-Grade Basketball Team

In the fall of 1963, my last year in Little League baseball, I had an opportunity to join our elementary school basketball team. We never had a school team before, but Jim Riggs's father, John, orchestrated the entry of a team in the Bridgeport School Recreational League. Our team was made up of seventh- and eighth-grade boys from our school. The team had mostly eighth-graders, so, again, I found myself in a rookie role.

We didn't need tryouts because the student body wasn't exactly beating the doors down to get on this team. We started to hold practices during lunch hour between morning dismissal at 11:40 and afternoon session bell at 1:15. I could look from my front yard through the yards across the street and see the front door of the school. Prior to basketball practice, I had plenty of time to go home for lunch every day. I would walk into the kitchen, where I would have a great sandwich and soup combination, or grilled cheese, or macaroni and cheese. Yes, my mother was the best cook in the world. Now I had to brown bag it! I really started to get an appreciation of the way people lived and what they were used to as I looked around at what everyone else brought for lunch every day. I never knew peanut butter was that popular. So much for peanut allergies! I also had to remember to take basketball practice gear and sneakers when I left the house in the morning.

During one of our practices, the coach gathered us around and started handing out a mimeographed sheet with the roster, player phone numbers, and game schedule on it. Our games were all going to be played at William Samuel Johnson School, which was in the heart of inner-city Bridgeport. I had never heard of the school and had no idea where it was. Fortunately, with our coach and one or two volunteers, we all managed to get to the host school on Saturday mornings. The week before our first game, everyone brought in a clean white T-shirt to practice. A few days later, the shirt was returned to us colored green with a white number heat-stamped to the back of it. We were also issued green and white basketball shorts (Thomas Hooker School's colors), and we were ready for game day.

Halfway through the season, it started to sink in that an organized team and formal coaching weren't going to increase my skill or my interest in this game right away. I was getting minimal playing time and usually just stood around on the court. The only difference was that I was indoors on a warm hard surface instead of standing outside with a heavy sweatshirt and muddy, frozen hands.

At this point, there were three paths you could take when you reach this fork in the road. First, you could elect to do something because you are good at it. If you were good at something, it would be fun and you would want to keep doing it. Second, you could do something that you enjoyed even if you were not good at it. This probably is true for two out of three golfers in the United States on any given weekend. Finally, you could decide to stop participating in a sport that you don't really enjoy and are not good at anyway. This is where I was with basketball; as a freshman in high school, I decided to pull the plug on basketball and to go back to my roots. I was going back to baseball.

Pony League Baseball

Still looking for the eternal baseball fix after graduating from Little League, the next step up was the Bridgeport Fire Department Pony League. Today, the same league is known as Babe Ruth League Baseball. At that time, the crossover from Little League to Pony League was like going from high school to college. These players were older, bigger, and stronger thirteen- to fifteen-year-olds. They threw faster, hit harder, and played rougher than Little League. The league itself expanded to include most of the city of Bridgeport. It was not unusual to have a teammate who had played on one of the other tournament teams we played in the Black Rock Tournament two years earlier. Case in point: I was on the same team with Woody Woodsen, the pitcher for the Black Rock Red Sox, who gave up the home-run ball to Lenny Harper. That was the hit that turned the tournament around for us. It's a small world!

The other social shake-up was the other side of that coin. Some of my closest teammates on the Little League Giants ended up on other teams we played against during the season. Even the playing field itself grew up. The diamond went from the traditional 60-foot base paths to the regulation 90 feet. Everything was bigger. The outfield on the home General Electric Field was 325 feet to the fence in left field and about 400 feet in straightaway center. This compared to the 210 feet of most Little League fields.

My Pony League experience got off to a slow and disappointing start. I came down with a nasty bout of the flu during March 1964 and missed a week of school and the weekends on both sides of that week. By the time I was back on my feet, most of the teams had conducted their tryouts and selected their players. The elite team in this league was the Royal Mets. Ed Conners, a Bridgeport legend as a sports figure, coach, administrator, and innovator, was the coach. This team managed to pick the cream of each Little League graduating class. The likes of Jim Riggs from the Braves and Dale Gestner, our ace Giant pitcher from my rookie year, were on this team. The Royals did have a "B" team and was a very good team in itself. Outstanding players such as our own Lenny Harper and John Blare were on that team, and they were a real force to be reckoned with.

My longtime best friend and Wiffle ball league partner, Billy, had not made either team, but he did find a home on the Vincent Brothers' team, sponsored by a home-heating company from our native city. Missing the tryouts was frustrating for me because I heard through the grapevine that if I had been there, I probably would have made the Royal Mets. As it was, I was a man without a country, a player without a team. I had just about resigned myself to the fact that my baseball days were over when one evening I received a call from the coach of Vincent Brothers. It seems that Billy's team was a player or two down on the roster and he had put in a good word for me. The coach was calling to invite me to try out for one of the slots.

Although I was finally happy to have a chance to play, the bloom was definitely off the baseball rose. These games were played just down the hill from the field I called home. The difference was there was no pomp and fanfare. No opening day parades, no bleachers, and no refreshment stand because very few parents and friends came to watch these games. On a good day you could catch the smell of french fries and hot dogs coming from the Little League field above. Metal spikes were a requirement, which was a little more intimidating and much closer to the Major League realism than the rubber spikes of Little League.

Gone, too, was the Major League uniform look of Little League. No authentic San Francisco Giant cap and uniform, no St. Louis Cardinal or Milwaukee Brave red, white, and blue. They were plain uniforms with local advertisements.

I suppose, in many respects, this was a situation that boiled down to pure desire to keep playing the game of baseball.

The games in this league also were isolated. Previously, in Little League, games were played on the same field, one right after another, and if you came before or stayed after your game, you could watch at least two other teams play. We had a sense of a league, standings, and a greater unit. You also had fans, parents, and other friends at the game. In the Pony League, the games were held in different locations, and it was just a more isolating feeling. I look back on the games that year and just remember specific incidents.

One Saturday afternoon, we were playing the Royal Mets, clearly the premier team in the league, and we were facing Dale Gestner. He had pitched us to the city championship in the last game in Black Rock. Dale was pitching one of his gems, being bigger and faster and more mature than his Little League days. In fact, he was pitching a no-hitter going into the fifth inning (Little League games are six innings long and Pony League games are seven innings).

Dale showed no signs of slowing down when I walked to the plate with two outs in the fifth inning. I let the first pitch go by, mostly because I couldn't see it, and the umpire called it a ball. The second pitch was even faster, and I swung and missed. Dale's next pitch came in and I swung much earlier, trying to match his blazing speed. I caught enough of the ball to get a small piece of it, and the ball chopped straight down on the plate; because of the hard flat surface, it bounced straight up in the air. Dale ran toward the plate and the catcher ripped his mask off, both waiting what seemed like forever for the ball to come down. By the time it did, I was at first base. That was the end of Dale's no-hitter. I tried not to look at the pitcher's mound while I was on first base, but I saw Dale look back over his shoulder with a smile that said, "Way to go, Jim." To add insult to injury, on the very next pitch, I took off from a short lead and stole second base, completely surprising the shortstop, second baseman, catcher, Dale, and my coach, since he gave no steal sign.

Stealing bases became the most exciting part of Pony League baseball for me. Runners could lead off the base in this league, as opposed to Little League. Without any coaching, I learned to read the pitcher's motions. I could take larger leads based on what I thought he was going to do. I would also watch the infielders, and if they weren't paying attention, I would steal. My most daring strategy was to steal second and, on the very next pitch, steal third. Stealing third is usually not done because the runner is already in scoring position at second base and usually not worth the risk. In a Major League game, that is probably true. In a Pony League game, even if the catcher had the ball, the third baseman was usually so far out of position that the catcher wouldn't throw the ball anyway. On the off chance that he did throw it, the timing is such that the ball usually wound up in left field.

These strategies didn't always work, and occasionally I was caught with egg on my face. On one such night we were playing Bridgeport Brass at Seaside Park. Seaside Park was the local beach. On a summer evening, you could smell the ocean, and it was always a little cooler there. The park had six baseball diamonds to play on. The infield dirt was reinforced with beach sand every year during the spring. Did you ever try to slide on beach sand? You can't. You just stop dead wherever you hit the ground.

In my second at-bat in this particular game, I turned a solid outfield line drive into a triple to start the inning. I pulled up at third base, and we had the beginning of a rally going. As the next batter came up to the plate, I took my normal lead off the base. The pitcher quickly and accurately whipped a throw over to the third baseman, and I made a feeble attempt to dive back. "You're out!" I heard the umpire say. I had been picked off third base. Getting picked off first base is bad enough, but being picked off third is a mortal sin.

Royal Treatment

I mentioned earlier that the Royal Mets were clearly the elite team in this league, and they had the pick of the prime Little League talent upon graduation. It was also prophetic that my bout with the flu at the beginning of the tryout period kept me off of that team. The ultimate irony in all this was that the Royal Mets were probably the team I performed the best against during my tenure in Pony League. There is no rhyme or reason to it, it just was.

In the late 1950s, the mediocre Detroit Tigers had a pitcher named Frank Lary. Frank was an average pitcher on a less-than-average team. However, in the middle of the Yankee dynasty, he would pitch well and beat the Yankees on a regular basis. This happened with such regularity that he was nicknamed the "Yankee Killer."

The Royal Mets were my Yankees. One of their best pitchers was a tall fireballer named Gerry Jepsen. Gerry's claim to fame was a high kick; he would rear back and throw with a lot of distracting arm and leg movement in his delivery. He usually gave up very few hits and often recorded double-digit strikeouts. I hit him very well, however, because the only thing I kept my eye on was his hand and the ball. I just made believe he was a pitching machine, and it worked very well. My only authentic home run in Pony League came off Mark Karagan, also a Royal Mets pitcher. I can't explain it, it just happened, and I kidded Mark for years about that one pitch.

Once I became a freshman in high school and crossed that bridge into adolescence, there were some interesting changes to my participation in sports. The first was that the competition was much better on a team and individual basis. As a sixth- and seventh-grader, I was used to being the fastest in the class. High school leveled that playing field very quickly. I was now in with older, more experienced guys who were just as fast as (if not faster than) I was.

Another change in my status as a player was that I began to participate in other sports. In addition to Pony League baseball, I also competed on the high school track team. After years of being coaxing by friends and family to run track because of my speed, I finally did so.

I hadn't been in my new high school a week when one morning in the hall, I was intercepted by Steve Minter, Harding High School's legendary football coach. Coach Minter stopped me and asked if I was Jim C and if I played football. I looked up in surprise, trying to figure out how he knew me and, more importantly, why he was so interested in me. About ten years prior to this, my cousin Mike was the quarterback of Harding during one of their most successful seasons. Not only did they beat everyone in sight, but they kicked the stuffing out of Bridgeport Central High School, 60–0, on Thanksgiving Day.

As a freshman, I weighed somewhere between 145 and 150 pounds, and as far as high school football was concerned, the only thing that Mike and I had in common was our last name.

Church League Basketball

Since my family's concern for my safety seemed to outweigh the coaches' motivation to have me on the team, I started to look to other venues to participate in the sports that I loved. In my sophomore year in high school, our church entered a team in the YMCA Interchurch Basketball League. We had a team of ten players that I came up through the Sunday school ranks with and presently went to the same high school together. I was reluctant to play this sport. which I was not particularly good at. However, I had a lot more playing time because of the many pickup games I was involved in. I had somehow gone from awful to acceptable in my basketball skills. That, and some peer pressure, was all it took to get me to the first practice.

A few practices into the preseason, we settled into a lineup and received our uniforms and schedules. Uniforms were red, white, and blue with satin shorts and shirts with stars on them. We looked like the Polish version of the Harlem Globetrotters and hoped we could live up to that image.

I was a substitute forward, and I was surprised early on at how much playing time I actually received, given the fact that I wasn't exactly burning the nets down with my shooting. I did discover a real "Aha!" moment that I eventually carried over to my coaching days. It was simple: "Skill to do comes from doing, so do it!" The coaches made sure that everyone was heavily involved in practices, and everyone received a fair amount of playing time regardless of skill level.

I became more involved in the game flow, and after a few games, I scored my first basket in an organized game. This was something I never managed to do when I was on the eighth-grade team. Yes, I hit my first two-pointer and then another and then another. There were games where I ended up with six to ten points as a substitute. The interesting thing about our team was that by midyear, we were undefeated; even our best player only averaged about fourteen to sixteen points. Before one of the games, I overheard a conversation between the league director and our coaches. The league director commented that even though we were in first place, no one on our team was in the top ten in scoring. It was true: with all the success we had had to date, no one was a standout. Every game we played had a different player, or combination of players, who excelled. It was a key ingredient in our success.

Between practices and games, we continued to gel as a unit, with the same fraternal feeling as the Little League Giants in my rookie year. Out of ten players on the roster, we had four sets of brothers, and then Danny Hamill and me. If there was a backbone to our team, it was Ed and Dave Rashen. Dave was an agile outside shooter, and his big brother Ed was our center. Ed wasn't particularly tall but he was built like a tank. He was also the varsity fullback on our high school team, so I probably painted the appropriate picture with that. If you were going up for a rebound against Ed, your initial tendency would be to just let him have it. It was a little like trying to take a bone away from a German shepherd.

We continued to play weekend games at the YMCA through the Thanksgiving and Christmas holidays. We were at that awkward age where we were too old to be driven by our parents and too young to drive. We often carpooled to get downtown to the games, and sometimes we took the local bus to the YMCA.

We finished the season at 12-0, with Black Rock Congregational coming in second in the Junior West Division (the same Black Rock that hosted the Little League tournament). Over in the Eastern Division, Greek Holy Trinity finished with an identical 12-0 record. Can you guess what was going to happen next? That's right, we couldn't possible have two undefeated league champs; we had to have an ultimate winner.

The stage was set for the Junior Division championship showdown. The YMCA gym was filled with as many people as you could get in there. There was also a running track that overlooked the gym floor, and spectators could watch from this elevated position. The downside of the track was that it created a ceiling effect in all four corners of the gym. That meant that you couldn't shoot from any one of the corners with any type of arc on the ball.

I was very nervous in the pregame warm-ups; it seemed that players on both sides were all wound up. It wasn't just two first-place teams but two undefeated teams, which probably increased the pressure. Someone was going home with their first loss at the end of the afternoon.

The game started, and players shuffled in and out quickly and on a regular basis. At halftime, we were tied 12–12, a very low scoring game. The defense prevailed on both sides. Although I didn't score in the game, I managed some defensive steals, pulled down a few rebounds, and generally just tried to contribute on defense.

At some point, it seemed like we stopped playing basketball and just turned into a free-for-all. With under a minute left, the score was tied at 22. I looked up at the clock. Two teams with 12-0 records tied 12–12 at halftime, and with a minute left, we were tied at 22–22. If ever there was a game that deserved to end in a tie, it was this one.

With less than thirty seconds left, there was another errant pass down in our end of the court. There was a mad scramble for the ball, bouncing around in the middle of this pile of humanity, similar to a group of seven-year-olds playing their first soccer game. The ball kicked out of the pile and into Dave Rashen's hands. Dave scooped up the ball and dribbled three or four times to get out of traffic. He pulled up and took a jumper from the top of the key. Swish! I couldn't believe how cleanly the ball went through the net. Later, Dave would recount the story, saying that if he had had a few seconds to think about the shot, he probably would have been lucky to hit the backboard. It was one of those times in sports where thinking is the worst thing you can do. Sometimes you just let your instinct, and your gut, guide your hands and feet.

We were ahead by two with under ten seconds. I guess we lost a few seconds after that because most of us on both sides were frozen in disbelief on how cleanly that shot went in. The Greeks, as we referred to them, tried to get the ball inbounds and quickly down the court to set up a last shot. There were few precious seconds left, and our coach screamed, "No fouls!" The game ended somewhere around half-court. We were the league champs at 13-0.

That year ended with our church giving us a banquet and jacket. It was at a time when as teenagers we were closely linked with the church. We had a basketball team, a youth group, Sunday school, and a bowling league. I was even Santa Claus for the first- and second-grade Sunday school kids. They all got to sit on my lap. My lap even got a visit from Ellen Hillman, my classmate and elf helper; life was indeed good!

As with Little League baseball, the second year in the basketball league was not close to the accomplishment and the drama of the first year. During our second year, the league expanded to a junior and senior division. Our junior championship team from the previous year was now in the senior division. The junior division was a portion of last year's team but with some new faces. The Rashens and other notables had moved on to the senior league.

I was in a unique situation, because as a December baby, I entered kindergarten when I was still four instead of five years old, which gave me one more year of eligibility with the juniors. I was able to play in both the junior and the senior games.

It was truly an interesting situation to be in. In one memorable game, I scored the first eight points of a game against Covenant Congregational. By the end of the game, I had twenty points in a 54–12 win for us. Both of our junior and senior teams had winning seasons, but neither made the postseason tournament, and my short-lived basketball career seemed to blend into the ever-increasing activities and pressures of a budding high school student.

Three Sports at Harding High School

My involvement in sports continued to swing from participation to watching sports and back again. As a freshman and sophomore, it was clear I wasn't going to be varsity material for football or basketball, but I loved going to the games. I especially loved the football games. Even the away games were within a reasonable distance, and going to the games not only satisfied my appetite for sports, it was a great social bonding opportunity. I did manage to adapt my schedule to participate on the bowling and tennis teams, no small feat since I learned both sports while on the team.

Harding Track

The problem with bowling and tennis was that, despite the fact that the teams were competitive, these weren't considered major sports. They were minor activities, ranked slightly above chess and student council. No one ever saw a cheerleader at a high school bowling match. Springtime, though, offered me my greatest challenge in high school. Should I go out for the baseball team, which was loaded with guys I had come up through Little League and Pony League?

I would be welcomed by those that knew my skill level and would acknowledge me as a major contributor. The alternative was to enter a new frontier and go out for the track team, with no knowledge of what that meant; my only source of confidence was knowing that I was fast.

I couldn't deny the call to try the unknown, and I gave up baseball for my first year in track. I realized that I needed to do some training prior to the first practice, so for the week before the tryout, I donned my best running shoes and ran around our neighborhood block once or twice. Little did I know at the time that running around the block to prepare for track was like swimming a few laps in the pool to train to swim the English Channel.

My sophomore year was my first year on the track team, and it was a real learning experience. I loved to run, and I was relatively fast, compared to the people I used to compete with. I needed to learn the strategy of the events, how to run them effectively, and which ones I could contribute the most to. You may wonder how much strategy there is to running. Depending on the race, sometimes not only your success but also your very survival depends on how smart you run the event. I never witnessed a better example of this than watching my youngest son years later at a championship meet in New Haven, Connecticut.

Their team's best sprinter had suffered a severe sprain a half an hour earlier in the 4 × 400 relay. Because John had already completed his event, the coach asked him if he could be a last-minute substitute in the 400-meter run. Being the gamer that he was, he said yes.

The runners were set, the gun cracked, and the race was on, with everyone flying out of the blocks as though the devil himself were chasing them. Now for those of you who remember the metric system, 400 meters is roughly the length of four football fields. It requires you to go from 0 to 60 miles per hour in as short a time as possible. Proper strategy dictates that you run the first 200 meters full speed and then break into a stride, conserving your energy for the last 100 meters. Because this was John's first attempt in the 400 meters, he didn't know this. I had positioned myself about 300 meters out on the track to cheer him on and offer support. To my absolute disbelief, as John went by me, he was still in an all-out sprint. I could only watch helplessly the last 100 meters. John sprawled toward the finish line, and as he crossed it, he instantly fell, hitting the track as though someone had shot him. He lay there motionless.

The coaches picked him up and carried him outside for some air (it was an indoor meet). John proceeded to lose about a quart of Gatorade, which he had consumed a short while before. In retrospect, if he had ever had a notion to run that race again, he mostly likely would spend some time learning how to run it more strategically.

Part of learning the ropes of a sport has to do with good communication and proper coaching. Unfortunately, my high school track career was lacking both. Our track coach was actually a minor league baseball pitcher. Although he had a competitive spirit and was always willing to help, he was not much help in teaching running and jumping techniques.

During my first year, however, I did learn another valuable skill. In the absence of formal training and experience, I could pick out the team members that were successful in their events and emulate them. If I could identify those actions, skills, and attitudes that made them excel at something, and I was able to duplicate and practice that skill, I could improve even without proper coaching.

I tried my best and did improve. High school track brought me to a crossroads in my own personal sports life. The issue was deciding that if I were going to really improve and make a major contribution, I had to make a much greater commitment in time and training, and even passion, to really see a difference. The other path was to continue at the same level to which I was performing and remain a runner-up.

I realized that participating in high school sports successfully required having an undeniable passion for the game. This passion would allow you to practice and work at your craft, long after the mediocre athletes had gone for pizza and retired for the night.

I settled into running the 100 and the 880 yards (or half mile) and competed in the long jump and high jump. I watch the high school competitors in those events today and smile. High jumpers land on incredibly thick foam rubber pads. Our high-jump pit was a combination of dirt and sand and sawdust. Whoever thought of that never jumped five feet over a bar and landed on his back. It might look like a soft landing, but I'm here to tell you it was not.

One of the things that hampered the team's success in my sophomore year was that after forty years, the school was finally getting a major facelift. The new renovation included a new music wing, a cafeteria, and an extra gym, and the existing building was refurbished as well. The downside of that was that our football field and track became a staging area for every dump truck and crane on the construction site. Potholes and stacks of construction material abounded and left us with no viable place to practice.

We finally received permission to practice on the track at the local university at Seaside Park. The campus was a good half hour away; we had to either take the bus or ride in a number of old cars, driven by juniors and seniors. We had to tie equipment such as poles and javelins to the roof of a car and hold on to them for dear life.

We tried our best to practice at the university's track. There were advantages to this location, in that our meets with Bridgeport Central and Bassick High School were scheduled on the same track. At first, the most grueling part of practice was running on the beach. The beach was a couple of miles long. Now although that is not very far, running that distance in sand is extra hard. Running two and a half miles in eighty-five-degree heat in the sand could be one of the definitions of "hell" in *Webster's Dictionary*. Over the next few weeks, the coach noticed that the ranks of runners had dropped and the number of field event members almost tripled. From that day on, the coach announced that everyone would be running the beach.

Running Home from Seaside Park

All the running began to pay off, and I was not only performing better, I was also enjoying running more and went for regular runs even over the summer. One such run that will live in my mind forever was on the Fourth of July 1967. We were all going to the beach for a party and to watch the fireworks. We grilled and had a good supply of drinks and even battled in a game of touch football. I had made up my mind that I was going to use this party as an opportunity to profess my feelings to Joyce, at that time the very soul of my existence. I'll never forget the way she looked that night, in her jean shorts, halter-top, sandals, and long brunette hair. If I make it to ninety years old, I will still remember what it was like to have that much trouble breathing.

As the evening wore on and the fireworks show concluded, the crowd started to disperse, with an impending thunderstorm looming on the horizon. I had turned down a few offers for a ride home because Joyce was still there with her friend Kathy, and I was hoping to provide her with some well-timed companionship at the end of the night. In one of those moments of life where joy and anticipation can turn to despair and disappointment, Joyce's mother drove up and she hopped into the car and drove away into the holiday crowd and the darkening sky.

I was almost completely out of transportation options at that point, with the aroma of hot dogs and gunpowder from the fireworks display filling the air. The first few drops of rain hit the beach sand. The rain striking me in the forehead seemed to say, "Stupid, stupid, stupid." I realized that I had made another idiotic decision in the name of love (or infatuation).

Filled with disappointment, embarrassment, and a general concern for my immediate safety, I just started to run toward the park exit. Since the traffic was bumper to bumper trying to get out of the park after the festivities, my hope was that one of my original offers for transportation (maybe even Joyce's mother) would see me and have pity. Such was not the case.

The farther I ran, the harder it rained. At that point, the decent thing for God to have done was to hit me with one of his best lightning bolts and end it all. As usual, he had other plans for me and was probably enjoying the show anyway.

Since this was 1967, I had no cell phone and, to the best of my recollection, was out of change for a pay phone, so I just kept running. The beach was two and a half miles long, and then the route home wound across the Housatonic River and past Washington Park and the WNAB radio studio. My run continued along Nobel Avenue and past the entrance to Beardsley Park, up Huntington Turnpike, past Thomas Hooker School, and on to my house. I never measured the distance, but it was in the neighborhood of six rain-soaked miles. I felt better by the time I got home.

I learned two important lessons that night:

- First: I could now run forever and actually enjoyed it.

- Second: A young lady in cutoffs will make an otherwise sane and intelligent man do unexplainable things.

Senior Year Track

Just as there was a maturation process from my first to my second year in Little League, so it was with track. My senior year, I was bigger and stronger and older than in my sophomore year. I was sprinting more regularly, now with better results. I was placing third, second, and sometimes first in my races, and I was doing even better in the field events.

We had some reasonably good success. I made it onto the relay team and had the distinction of being the only Caucasian runner in that group of four. In the meet against Fairfield Prep, Curtis Franks, who ran the third leg of the relay, dropped the baton on a turn. He jammed on the brakes, ran back, and picked up the baton, and we still ended up winning the heat. Now that's fast!

I ran the 220-yard dash against Bunnell High School. Bunnell's track had a unique layout for the 220: it was a straightaway. The first hundred yards of this event usually goes straight and then the track curves. With this particular track, the entire 220 yards was as straight as an arrow. From the starting line, it looked like 220 miles. Despite the straightaway's visual intimidation, I ran the best 220-yard race of my life, finishing second with a personal best time.

The End of My Track Career

By the time our team was a third of the way into my senior season, the construction contractors completed their work on the track. Although we couldn't use the field for meets yet, we could practice there, and because we didn't have to travel thirty minutes in both directions, we gained more practice time.

One unseasonably hot day, we were practicing just outside the school gym on the track. The sprinters were running repeated sprinting drills. Inside the gym, the cheerleaders were conducting tryouts. I was sprinting with a group of three others, rounding the near turn by the door of the gym. We were dripping with sweat and my head was pounding from the heat. I was flying around the last turn with the pack when I felt the ground give out from under me. I had suffered a serious case of heat exhaustion that sent me collapsing on the hot gravel of the track. I lay there motionless. My head was pounding, my legs were burning from cuts and scratches, and I could hear faint voices. When I did manage to open my eyes, I looked up to see the frantic face of Joyce and her friends along with the trainer. Joyce was wiping my face dry with a T-shirt, and I realized that this was the reason God hadn't hit me with a lightning bolt on the Fourth of July. I thought I was dead and was looking up at an angel.

A few days later, we were running conditioning drills on the football field. During these drills, everyone ran in a single file, and the runner at the back of the line pulled out and sprinted up to the front of the line. It was my turn at the end of the pack, and as I started to pull out and accelerate, I tripped over one of the irrigation pipes. I was extremely lucky that I didn't break anything, but within a few minutes my foot was swollen beyond recognition.

After a trip to the hospital emergency room, I had to miss the last four meets of the season. I still attended team meetings and practices, hobbling around on crutches, with a bedroom slipper on my right foot. At the last team meeting of the year, there was a special presentation that I will never forget. Because of my injury, I was a few points shy of qualifying for my letter in track. The team and the coaches had voted that I should receive the letter anyway and presented it to me at that last meeting. The letter meant more to me coming from my peers than if I had earned it in the conventional way.

The day before graduation, all the seniors were in the school auditorium for our last graduation rehearsal. We had just received our yearbooks and were busy signing each other's books. At one point I looked up to see Joyce, standing a few feet away, writing in someone's book. She looked up and caught me looking over and smiled. I walked over and sheepishly asked if she would sign my book. She said sure and wrote:

> *Jim, may you have the best of everything in life . . .*
> *you deserve it.*
>
> *Love, Joyce*

We were headed off to different colleges, but I wanted to ask if I could keep in touch. I didn't want this to be the last time I would ever see her. As I fumbled through one last attempt to keep hope alive, it occurred to me. The entire time I had known her, I was more worried about rejection than about spending some time getting to know her as a friend and giving her an opportunity to know me. I realized that I didn't have much of a case on which to build a relationship.

We went our separate ways, and I made a promise to myself that day that I would never be that unprepared for life again. To this day, I owe a great deal of my good fortune and success to that one improbable moment. I lost a lot that day, but I gained so much more as a result of it.

Sports in the Real World

As a teenager, my participation in sports seemed to fit right in with my life. It was not only a form of recreation but also a way of socializing, bonding, and learning life lessons. Once I graduated from high school, the landscape of my life seemed to shift again.

The academic pressure of college significantly decreased the amount of time I had to participate in sports. Sports at the college level demanded even more of an athlete's time than any previous sports commitment I had ever encountered. High school friends slipped away to different colleges in other states. Sports became more social and less competitive, from pickup basketball games and company softball games to occasional bowling outings and tennis on a summer night. At one of these tennis matches, I made a date with Beth, and she eventually became my wife.

Art's American Softball

There was one more return to the team sport that I loved the most, as a young adult soon to be married. I had a good friend in high school who had transferred from Richmond, Virginia, in our sophomore year. Dave Nash was our resident southern boy, and we even called him "Reb" after the Rebels of the Civil War Confederacy. He fit right into our circle of friends, which spoke a lot about his flexibility. Since he attended college locally as I did, we stayed in touch after graduation.

Dave called me up one night and asked me if I wanted to play on his softball team that spring. I didn't even wait until he finished the sentence before accepting, and he added that there would be a practice at the end of the week. We went together to the first practice, and it was a wise move. Even though I was an established native of Bridgeport, I knew no one on this team. In fact, it wasn't Dave's team at all, but a group of mechanics from a local garage called Art's American.

I was apparently there to fill a miscellaneous slot if another player either had his car repossessed or was too drunk to find his glove on game day. Oh, they were friendly enough, but I didn't exactly fit in. Gradually, they worked me into the lineup at a variety of positions, playing one or two innings and getting one at-bat if I was lucky. The frustrating part was that this team hadn't come close to winning a game by midseason. Since it just felt good to be in a uniform at twenty-five years old, I went to every game and played when I could.

One Sunday, we had a game with Mickey's Bar scheduled at eleven o'clock. Now the unfortunate part about Sunday morning games is that they almost always followed Saturday nights. Saturday nights, to this collection of party boys, meant drinking heavily until 3:00 a.m. and eventually getting physically removed from the establishment they were occupying. This particular episode was another one of my life's examples where a great opportunity was cleverly disguised as an impossible situation. Out of a roster of twelve, we only had nine players this particular Sunday. I started the game at second base.

I'm not sure why, but despite our poor turnout, we played well and the score was tied, 3–3, in the top of the seventh and last inning. Maybe it was because the opposing team had been at the same bar the previous night. I didn't have time to look a gift horse in the mouth.

We came out to bat in the top of the seventh. Our first batter flied out to left. I was the next batter and, after taking two high pitches for balls, caught a decent pitch on the outside part of the plate and sent a line drive between the right and center fielders. I rounded first base and looked out to see that the outfielders had barely caught up to the ball. I knew this was going to be at least a double. I decided to go for it and never stopped when I got to second base. I did take a quick look at the third-base coach in time to see him deep in conversation with a cute little blonde with a heart tattooed on her arm. Realizing he was going to be of no use, I turned on the afterburners, and by the time the ball reached the infield, I was sliding into third.

This new development created an interesting situation for us. With one out, we had the go-ahead run on third base. Now, sound baseball knowledge would dictate that the next batter up should hit the ball to the right side of the infield. This would give the runner on third (me) the best chance of scoring. However, baseball knowledge, common sense, and, yes, even sobriety had little to do with this team. The next batter bounced the first pitch right to the third baseman. He caught the ball cleanly and took a quick look at me. I was a few feet off the bag, and when he looked over, I took a few steps back toward third base, giving him my best "I'm not going anywhere" look.

This was another one of those times where I knew what I was going to before I did it. In that split second after the third baseman decided I wasn't going anywhere, he threw the ball to first base to get the sure out. As he let the ball go, I took off like a shot for home plate. You could hear the entire team screaming, "Go home, go home!" By the time the first baseman had the ball and fired it to the catcher, I arrived at home plate about the same time the ball did, and in a cloud of dust, I looked up to see the faint image of the umpire with his hands spread apart. "Safe, safe!"

All I remember was being lifted up off the ground in a sea of red Art's American shirts. The bench had cleared; in a temporary celebration, we all relished the fact that we now had our first lead of the year, 4–3. The celebration was short lived, because the next batter grounded out and the reality of playing the last half of the inning loomed in front of us.

As we took the field for the home half of the seventh inning, two things occurred to me. First was that we had never been ahead in any game going into the last inning. Second was how quickly teams managed to score four and five runs against us. In this case, they only needed two runs to win the game. I decided to keep both of those revelations to myself.

The first batter up hit a towering pop-up in back of third base. Our third basemen made an easy play of it for the first out. The second batter singled to center, and I braced myself for the worst. With a runner on first, the next batter hit a sharp ground ball to me at second. The ball took an erratic bounce on the infield and hit me in the chest. I kept the ball in front of me and saw that our shortstop was not going to make it in time for the throw. I took the sure out, throwing to first. Two outs, runner on second.

All they needed was a single to the outfield and they would tie it up. Again we were faced with undeniable baseball logic. With a runner at second, the book says not to hit the ball on the left side of the infield, either to the shortstop or the third baseman or even the left fielder. To give the runner on second the best chance to score, you need to hit the ball to the right side, behind the runner. The right-handed batter stepped to the plate, and I instinctively inched toward first base to favor the right side. The batter knew what he was doing. He hit a hard ground ball toward the gap between me and the first baseman. I made a desperation dive, lying flat on my stomach, and felt the ball hit my glove. I steadied myself in a kneeling position, picked the ball out of my glove, and threw a waist-high strike to the first baseman. Three outs and game over, Arts American 4, Mickey's Bar 3.

Although this was only a men's recreational league, the game was a turning point for me. I was accepted as an honorary member of this grease monkey fraternity. I played on that team two more years, and by the third year, I was elected captain.

We played many games over the next three years, and as I edged closer to the thirty-year-old milestone, I noticed something interesting. If there was any part of the game that had eroded for me, it was not the physical but the mental side of the game. I was stronger than I had ever been and still very fast, considering I wasn't eighteen anymore. Still, I found myself making mental errors that I never used to make.

We were playing a double header one weekend and the first game was with a mediocre team with older players. We won the first game; I had a few hits and scored a few times. In the second game, I was on second base and the batter singled to left center field. I raced around third base and headed for home. Halfway down the third-base line headed toward home, I felt something go flying past my left ear; it felt like a shell from a howitzer canon. Alas, it was the ball! I was out at home by three feet. Instead of a middle-aged bank teller in left field, as in the first game, there was a six-foot, three-inch Jamaican with muscles on top of muscles sticking out of cut sleeves on his uniform top. If I had managed to assess the defense between the first and second game, I probably would have stopped at third on that play.

It was while playing for Art's American that I met Beth, my wife of thirty-five years now. Beth often arrived at Seaside Park in her floppy hat and shorts and sandals, looking for the entire world like a southern belle. Who knew that the very field where I was picked off third in a Pony League game and ran my first half-mile race in high school would eventually hold such treasures?

Another Gas Station Team

I had enough success as part of Art's American to now be noticed by other teams. My sister Cindy was dating another weekend warrior during that time. John Kline was an avid softball player whose enthusiasm exceeded his skill level. Nevertheless, John attended every game and gave it his all. His team also had attendance problems, and John invited me to play a few games with them. I was fortunate to have a few good games with them early on and worked my way into a starting role, this time in the outfield. The team was Turnpike Shell. Yes, another gas station!

We had a reasonably good year. I missed some of the season with minor surgery. When I returned a few weeks later, I picked up right where I left off. In fact, in my first game back, I had four hits in four times at bat, including a two-run home run. The team joked that I should have surgery more often.

Although I only knew a few players on the Shell team, I was quickly accepted in the starting lineup. I was the starting center fielder, and for someone closing in on thirty years old, I was still fast enough to cover a lot of outfield. My hitting was improving also. In a slow-pitch softball game, I eventually trained myself to hit the ball just about anywhere I wanted if I waited for the right pitch. I also used my speed and knowledge about the other team to turn singles into doubles and doubles into triples. I was sliding feet first and head first, and diving after balls hit into the outfield. I was having as much fun as a six-year-old playing in the dirt.

Playing hard at any age has a price. In one particularly hard-fought game, I came away with some nasty burns on my leg. Postgame assessment revealed the entire side of my right leg sustained a serious sliding burn; much of the skin was torn off and scratched deep enough to bleed. We were beginning a series of postseason tournament games, and there wasn't really time for me to heal before the next game. Beth was a registered nurse at the time and came to my rescue. She dressed the sizeable wound and wrapped it in gauze and an ace bandage from knee to hip. Although it was somewhat restricting, I was ready to play.

One of the interesting things about team sports is that your personal skill level is always relative to the rest of the team on which you're playing. During my career as a baseball and softball player, I played every position on the field and batted in every slot in the lineup. On some teams, I was a nobody, batting as far down in the order as they could put me. On other teams, I was more of a power hitter, batting in the fourth or fifth position. For this particular team, I actually led off, hitting first. I was making good contact and could always be counted on to get on base. I was also the fastest runner on the team, and it was good to have someone like that on base when the power hitters came up.

To start our next game, I stepped up to the plate as the leadoff batter, with my freshly bandaged leg, looking to get the game started on the right foot. The second pitch was letter-high and on the outside part of the plate. I hit the ball squarely and sent a hard line drive about three feet over the second baseman's head for a leadoff single. It was a great start, and I had a feeling I was going to have a good game. The next batter followed with a sharp ground ball to the shortstop. It was hit hard enough to be a tailor-made double-play ball. I had a good jump off first base and knew it was going to be a close play. The shortstop threw a strike to the second baseman. I knew I was going to be out, and the only thing to do was to prevent him from throwing on to first for the double play. I instinctively hit the ground in a long, hard slide, obstructing the view and the throw of the second baseman.

When the dust cleared, the second baseman was on the ground, still holding the ball, and the runner at first was safe. As the dust continued to clear, I looked down to see significant wet red spots coming through my uniform pants. The hard slide had pretty much torn Beth's expert bandaging job into an unrecognizable mess. I tried to explain this to my irate nurse (and soon-to-be wife), telling her that years of sports experience and instincts had taken over in a split second, replacing all rational thought and logic.

I limped off the field, and Beth and I quickly adjourned to a nearby ladies' room. I stood on the toilet in the stall while Beth used paper towels to wash sand out of bleeding leg wounds (let me tell you how good that felt) and redress the wound with toilet paper and tape. I was able to get back into the game, and we eventually won the game and moved on in the tournament.

Paying It Forward

I enjoyed this season and did well. The only downside was that as I continued to play more, it was at the expense of John, Cindy's boyfriend, who sat on the bench while I played his position. If there was anyone on the team besides me who loved this game, it was

John. I knew it was hard to sit out any game, but the tournament was especially painful for him. We had a night game during the tournament, and I had never had a chance to play under the lights prior to this. It was interesting getting used to hitting and fielding in those conditions.

As we prepared to take the field, we assembled in the dugout as the manager read off the starting lineup. John hung on every name, hoping there was a spot for him. Batting sixth, batting seventh, and batting eighth, still no mention of John. He put his glove down on the bench and sat back in disappointment; I was probably the only one this bothered. As the first inning unfolded, I couldn't help sneaking a look over at our bench, watching John try to keep his spirits up in case he was called on. I couldn't do this anymore.

A few pitches later, the batter lined a single to left center field. I ran toward the left fielder and he ran toward me. I cut the ball off and threw into second base, holding the runner to a single. I never really planned what happened next, I just thought of it then and there. While jogging back to my position, I started to limp. My limp turned into a hobble, and then I called timeout and sat down on the outfield grass, holding my ankle. The umpire came out along with Ken, our shortstop, and Phil, the left fielder. My teammates helped me to my feet and I limped back to the bench. I slumped onto the pine bench, grimacing in apparent pain. Almost on cue, I could hear the manager say, "John, take center field." John hopped up like he had been sitting on a hot plate. As he started to run out onto the field, he stopped dead and looked back over his shoulder. To this day, I don't remember much of that last game, but one thing I will never forget is the look on John's face. If you can possibly imagine a combination of childlike joy, concern, and gratitude rolled into one expression, you have some idea of what it was like.

I am sure I was the only one who knew I didn't need an ice bag. There was nothing wrong with my ankle that watching John play the rest of the game couldn't fix. He was, after all, the one who recommended me for this team. He had allowed me one more season in the sun as I came closer to the end of my playing days. It was my tribute to him, my "thank you" in a gesture of respect and love for the game. It was a game I truly enjoyed. I will never forget it.

I believe that there are opportunities in life, in and out of sports, to "pay it forward," to share a good deed, a kind gesture, even a smile and a word of encouragement. It could be the opportunity that someone was looking for when they had no place else to turn. It could be just a temporary courtesy, a turning point in that person's life. It's not yours to decide or to take credit for or pay back. It will be included in a short list of the things that truly matter as you travel down life's road. I will personally always look for an opportunity to pay it forward.

Milestones and New Priorities

These teams of weekend warriors were starting to break up faster than a sailboat in a hurricane. Teammates were changing jobs, getting engaged and married, moving to better opportunities. Recreational sports slipped on the priority list, below securing a better job and starting a family. It was a bittersweet time. It was time to move on but always with an eye on one more chance to stand in the outfield or stand on the basketball court and see the net pop on a twenty-footer. It was more than the sports too. It was the fraternal bond of competition, the joy of the game, and being in the hunt.

The Chestnuts Softball Team

In September 1977, I married my best friend, nurse, and VP in charge of bandaging. I was working in Stamford and going to graduate school in New Haven. Beth was working at a veteran's hospital, and we were living in a small starter home. There were no team sports on the horizon, but Beth and I spent our first date on the tennis court and continued to steal court time when we could. We also joined a bowling league, sharing the fun of sports and the excitement of competition.

By 1981, we had taken the plunge and bought a new home in the neighboring town of Oxford. A year later, our firstborn, Matthew, came into our lives, and suddenly we were lucky to get a few hours of sleep, let alone show up for a team practice. As we settled into our new life, we started to meet our neighbors and other young families in the immediate area. One night, during a neighborhood get-together, one of our friends mentioned that he and his cohorts at the town hall were considering starting a men's softball league.

It didn't take much to get commitments from a dozen thirty-something sports enthusiasts and warhorses of Little League, high school, and college sports. We entered a team and ordered uniforms and caps with our team name, the Chestnuts. Now before you start doing extensive research on the significance of a chestnut in the annals of sports, I'll say that it was the name of our street. There was really no deeper meaning than that.

Our team had no elaborate practices or strategies. This was just a group of new husbands and fathers who threw a glove and a pair of cleats in the car along with a brief case and a lunch box and said, "Honey, I'll be home a little late tonight."

We managed to play a fifteen-game schedule and came in first place, only losing one game during the course of the season. This was a short-term league because the players themselves were short term, always with other commitments. One of the significant takeaways of this season for me was that some of the games were played at the Babe Ruth field at Posypanko Park, home of the Oxford Little League. Talk about coming full circle! It was a place where the green grass, brown dirt, and white chalk lines were resurrected from 1962. It was a place where the Stars and Stripes fluttered over the large scoreboard, the refreshment stand, and the bleachers.

The Chestnuts were just one dying ember in a wonderful collection of my days as a player. It was the last gasp for me as a player; with the exception of a few benefit softball games and United Way golf tournaments, my playing days were at an end. After the last Chestnuts game that year, I sat on the bleachers, took off my cleats, and looked over the fence at a Little League game that was going on. In a bittersweet flash, I realized that the Chestnuts had led me to my next calling. This calling would provide even more golden memories as my family soon expanded to three boys. I was headed for a welcomed transition from player to coach.

CHAPTER 4

From Player to Coach

During the course of my lifetime, my intimate relationship with sports has gone through three distinct phases.

The first phase is really just watching the game, the competition, the drama of the sport. Whether it is baseball, football, basketball, hockey, or golf, there is a certain draw that is unmistakable. I have been in a sports bar and seen people watching the Super Bowl who clearly have no real clue as to the game's rules or purpose. Yet these people, male and female, young and old, are still caught up in the excitement and drama of the game.

The second phase was a logical extension of watching: playing. If I watched and enjoyed a sport and learned enough, I naturally wanted to try my hand in it. It is a natural desire to want to experience participation and live it just as the athletes that I watched and admired did. I may not be as good as Tiger Woods or Tom Brady, but I can develop my own level of enjoyment and proficiency.

The third phase was coaching. I became a coach for two reasons. The first was that I truly believed that no one on earth could give my three sons the same level of enthusiasm, knowledge, and expertise in baseball and basketball as I could. The second, and probably even more important, was that I wanted to bridge the gap that I was beginning to notice. This gap between the childhood innocence and excitement that I had experienced as a young boy and the waning values, the "me" instead of "team." The attitude that said, "Let me show the world how great I am," this approach to competition, was beginning to sour my enthusiasm as a sports fan. Yes, I wanted to share, to give back, but I was also doing it for selfish reasons. I wanted to extend the feeling a little longer. I wanted to have one more day in the sun on a hot July afternoon, stomping the dirt out of my baseball cleats and finishing off the last bite of ballpark hot dog.

It was a different town, a different field, and different players in uniform. Coaching, for me, was the next logical extension of my legacy as a sports fan. If I did a decent job, maybe I could develop some real sports fans from this new crop of rookies.

What Is T-Ball?

My oldest son, Matt, is now a thirty-year-old father himself; he was the first of my sons to enter into the wonderful world of sports. When he was seven years old, we decided to enroll him in T-ball so that he could participate and socialize with his classmates. If you are not familiar with T-ball, it's the same game as baseball except that the ball is hit off of a three-foot-high rubber tee. If you have ever seen a six- or seven-year-old pitch a baseball, you'll know why the Tee is critical to this age group. If we left it to a seven-year-old pitcher, the game would not be measured in innings; it would be measured in weeks.

The day of registration came and we filled out forms and wrote out the checks for the various league fees. If you hung around the registration table for more than a few minutes, you noticed that there were actually two lists on the table. There was a list for players and one for potential coaches. Although the player list was overflowing, the coaches' list was as unpopulated as the Mojave Desert. Before I could imagine what it might be like to coach twelve seven-year-old T-ball players, my wife chimed in, "Jim, you would make a good coach, why don't you sign up?" This is always the case with my wife; soon, I was sitting at a coaches' meeting at the school.

If I was so experienced with baseball, then why was I so nervous at this meeting? I quickly realized that 80 percent of the parents who came to the coaches' meeting knew less baseball than I did, and if they could coach, how hard could it be? I was issued an equipment bag, balls, bats, and a catcher's mask (there is no pitcher in a T-ball game but there is a catcher; somebody's got to watch home plate). I was also given twelve tiny shirts and twelve tiny hats along with a roster, schedules, first aid kit, and the phone numbers of the league officers. Just when my anxiety level started to rise again, I received one more gift. It was a T-ball mom, one of the mother volunteers, to help with the logistics of schedules and uniforms. I realized that if I played my cards right, I could probably pass along some of the coaching duties to her. Yes, this was going to work out. I had another potential sports fan to develop.

As my first season of coaching progressed, I was facing two important challenges. The first was that my responsibilities to this team were going beyond just teaching them baseball. There were schedules to be managed, paperwork to be processed, pictures and seasonal activities to be arranged, and parents I needed to satisfy.

The second significant realization was that I was going to have to take twenty years of baseball knowledge and experience and distill it into a form that was educational, fun, and yet easy to understand for a seven-year-old. This was a challenge for me. Every practice, every game, and every meeting taught me as much as I was trying to teach the team.

One of the interesting things about trying to relate to seven-year-old boys and girls was the fact that kids, even at this age, will rise to a certain level of expectation that you set, even if it is unintentional and somewhat unrealistic. Case in point: Once I had established the concept of infielder and outfielders and what they were supposed to do, we began to practice hitting the cutoff man (or player, since there were girls in this league). Simply put, when the ball is hit to right field, while the outfielder chases the ball, the second baseman runs into the outfield, about halfway between the right fielder and second base. The idea is that when the right fielder finally picks up the ball, he or she throws the ball to this cutoff player, who is significantly closer than the rest of the infielders. The cutoff player gets the ball and throws it to one of the infielders covering second base. If done correctly, it is a faster and more accurate way of getting the ball from the far reaches of the outfield back to civilization.

Well, we practiced this drill religiously along with throwing, catching, hitting, and other skills (other skills included remembering to bring your glove to practice and running the bases in the right direction). During one of our first games, the league director stopped by and watched for an inning. As luck would have it, one of the other team's players hit a ball into the outfield. Our enthusiastic outfielder took off after the ball with as much speed as a seven-year-old can muster, even throwing her glove at the ball to slow it down. She finally caught up to it just about the time one of our infielders miraculously reached the right position to take a relay throw. Almost on cue, the outfielder threw the ball into the cutoff player, who managed to gather it up in his glove and threw it to the approximate area of second base (give or take ten feet).

The director walked up to me during a break in the action and, with a somewhat condescending smile, said, "Coach, don't you think these kids are a little young to be doing relays? We don't usually teach them that until Little League." Well, apparently I'd missed the memo. The only ones who didn't know were the seven-year-olds on my team. They were doing just fine.

This was only one day out of a ten-year coaching experience for me, but what I learned made me a better coach and, even more importantly, a better father. Providing opportunities for kids to learn and explore, while raising the bar a little with optimistic expectations, creates wonderful opportunities to achieve the unexpected.

The Parents

No matter how much baseball you know and how great you are relating to children, an important piece of coaching is communicating with the parents. Seven years old can be a tough time to start playing baseball, because it is a sport that can put you in the spotlight at any time. When your child plays soccer, they can blend into a pile of small children, kicking and laughing wildly, and everyone has fun. In T-ball, when the ball is hit to you and only you, or when you are standing at home plate ready to hit the ball, all eyes are on you. As a coach, I tried to teach teamwork and working together just as much as individual skills. I was amazed when I realized how intently parents watched and listened to me as I did this.

Coaching is a real commitment; to do it right, at any level, it is more of a commitment than you may think. Most parents have full-time jobs and other children's activities; they struggle just to get their little outfielder to a game, let alone be able to stay and watch. They certainly cannot deal with the logistical landslide of coaching. There are certain perks to being a coach. First, you get to wear a baseball cap. Second, you get free hot dogs and a drink at the concession stand after every game. French fries, too, if you win! The greatest perk in coaching, though, is taking the equipment bag home. The bag consists of six bats, eight baseballs, three bases, a catcher's mask, and catcher's equipment. Based on how well your team remembers their personal equipment after a game, you usually have one or two extra baseball gloves and maybe a package or two of bubble gum.

The bag was a necessity for games and team practices, but it also received a great workout at home on our off days. The boys and I looked for any opportunity to take the bag out into our front yard, set up the tee and bases, and voilà! Instant baseball game.

These practice games gradually increased in frequency, and we even had friends and neighbors join us occasionally. No matter who was playing, we always had fun and the boys refined their skills without even realizing it. That practice really started to show during games.

T-Ball to Minors

Once I made the commitment to coach, there was no turning back. My three sons were spaced only a few years apart, and as one finished a level of baseball and graduated to the next, another one would come up right behind him. While most parents only committed to coaching for a year or two, I continued. In the years that followed, I found myself coaching both T-ball and Minor League baseball.

With each advance into the next age group came new challenges. In the case of Minor League, the most significant difference was pitching. In a T-ball game, the ball sat on a tee in front of you. You could position the tee higher or lower, and the batter had as long as they wanted (within reason) to hit the ball. Minor League baseball introduced the concept of pitching into the game. That became a double-edged sword. The batter now had to stand up there and hit a ball traveling at some rate of speed. Timing became an issue. As a coach, I needed to teach a new set of skills. These batters began to practice when to swing at the ball for optimum probability of contact. Another batting skill was pitch selection. The batter was not obligated to swing at every pitch, since there were good pitches and bad pitches.

While we are on the subject of good and bad pitches, it brings me to the other side of that double-edged sword. Since T-ball used a tee, there was no need for pitchers. In the Minor League, we had to develop a few pitchers who could consistently throw the ball from the pitcher's mound to the catcher with reasonable accuracy.

The combination of pitchers with poor accuracy and batters who were afraid to swing at pitches made for very long games. As a precaution against these potential marathons, the league had an eight batter-per-inning maximum. A team stayed at bat until they made three outs or they had completed eight batters. There were many times where we had sent eight batters to the plate and there were still no outs.

The combination of inaccurate pitching and tentative batters also created a remarkable lack of activity in the early minor league games. Hitting the ball into fair territory was an oddity, and this created a whole new set of opportunities. Because of this lack of activity, it wasn't uncommon to have these young players slip into lapses of inattentive behavior. I had one young right fielder who solved his boredom problem by sitting down in the outfield. He would then take his cap off and put it in his lap. While the game was going on, he would methodically fill his cap with grass and leaves that he pulled from the outfield turf on which he sat. On the odd chance that the ball was hit in his direction, he couldn't be in a worse position to make the play.

Another major difference between T-ball and Minor Leagues was in the lineups and batting orders. In T-ball, everyone played at the same time. There were no positions and no substitutions. We filled the field with little ones and let the chips fall where they may. When it came time for your team to bat, we would sit them all in a single straight line along the baseline. One by one they would come up and take their turn batting until everyone had had a turn, and then we would switch and the other team would bat. In Minor League, you had a twelve- or thirteen-player roster, and only nine could play at a time. The lineups and batting order were captured in a scorebook, and as a coach, I was responsible for creating a reasonable lineup and ensuring that everyone played at least two innings per game.

As the season progressed, I had to evaluate our talent inventory. This was not only to see which players needed practice and instruction in specific skills, but also to identify their strengths. This information helped me decide where to place these future stars during a game. Some were naturally better throwers, hitters, and runners than others. Based on that information, I began to put them into positions that made sense not only for their development, but to ensure that the games were completed before the two-hour rule was evoked. Without these types of time limits on Minor League ball, some of these games might still be going on.

The position of catcher was also a maiden voyage into the unknown. Since T-ball had no pitcher, all the catcher did was guard home plate. With a pitcher, we needed a catcher, considering that 98 percent of the pitches went by the batter anyway. Because we needed a catcher, we also needed catcher's gear. A mask, chest protector, and shin pads were essential. If you are a parent, you probably know that on a good day, it takes an average eight- or nine-year-old a half hour just to get dressed in regular school clothes. Adding this baseball suit of armor was indeed an interesting challenge. Some of the kids wanted to be the catcher, just to wear the "stuff."

Catching is also not as easy as it looks. It's a study in timing and judgment. Part of the judgment is positioning yourself far enough behind the batter to avoid being clubbed if he finally decides to swing at a pitch. It is also an exercise in concentration. It is very difficult to watch a pitch come in and block out the batter and his swing enough to catch the ball.

The intriguing thing about all this for me as a coach was that eventually I had to break all these functions down into small, teachable segments. I had to analyze them and put myself in the shoes of someone learning it for the first time. This was especially difficult because I had been playing baseball a long time; you get to a point where performing these skills becomes automatic. You stop thinking about how to do it and instinctively just do it when the situation arises.

Because of the way my sons were gradually introduced into the baseball program, I was gradually introduced into the coaching ranks. As my oldest graduated from T-ball to Minors, I was, at first, a T-ball coach and then a father/spectator in the Minors. Gradually, I took on the role of assistant coach in the Minors, helping the head coach. As the seasons progressed and fathers and sons moved up to the next level, I took over the reins as head coach with assistants helping me.

This was about the time I started coaching two teams, one T-ball team (with my middle son, Jimmy) and one Minor league team (with Matt). That meant two bags of equipment, two schedules, two sets of parents, and all the administrative hoops to jump through. I loved it, though! Next to playing, I couldn't be more engrossed in the sport I loved.

Opening Day

Opening day of the 1992 season was on a beautiful spring day. I had two sons on two different teams (and one three-year-old who was sure to follow in his brothers' footsteps). The uniforms and schedules were distributed, and the entire league was assembled for opening day ceremonies. The field was manicured, the lines were painted, and team pictures were taken. The bleachers were filled with parents and friends, while volunteer mothers buzzed around the overstocked refreshment stand, trying to serve the triple line of siblings and parents who had come to join in the day's festivities. The sound of the PA system and the smell of french fries, hot dogs, and fried dough filled the air.

Prior to a full day's schedule of games, we all assembled on the field for opening day exercises. T-ball, Minor League, and Major League teams all lined up in neat colorful rows facing home plate. After a prayer and a welcome by local officials, we all stood at attention with our caps off for the national anthem. As the first few notes of "The Star Spangled Banner" bellowed from the PA system, I couldn't help but think back almost thirty years to the day of my first opening day of Little League. Once again I recalled the church breakfast and the parade on Boston Avenue to the Little League field. I could see the pennants waving one more time and see the refreshment stand of the Park City Little League. For a brief minute, these two memorable events became one. I felt good knowing that in some small way, I was able to share one of the warmest memories of my childhood with my young sons and wife. I wasn't sure if they saw it the same was as I did. I didn't know if it would be as memorable in years to come; I was just happy that we were all sharing this day together.

Minors to Majors

A season or two passed, and the baseball landscape continued to change. My oldest son, Matt, had graduated into the eleven- and twelve-year-old Major Division. My T-baller, Jimmy, had moved from T-ball to Minors, and John finally broke into the T-ball ranks.

Although I was just a spectator in the Majors, I was head coach for Jimmy's Minor League team, and I took on another T-ball coaching assignment with John's team. With all three sons participating, it was no surprise that we spent many of our spring and summer evenings at Posypanko Field. Ironically, this was the same field where I played my very last game ten years earlier.

Matt was the first to break in to the ranks of the Major Leagues. I had not had the opportunity to coach at the Major level and was content to stand by the fence and watch Matt make his debut with the Pirates. He had a good, level-headed, and even-tempered coaching staff (which is rare in this day and age, and I was very grateful). I would run from game to game, to fence to game, just to take it all in. I gradually learned everyone's name and became more involved in the administration of the league. There were even days when I jumped into the refreshment stand, slung burgers and fries, and passed out candy and gum.

The biggest coaching challenge during those days was effectively relating to age groups between eight and twelve years old. At some point, coaching a T-ball game and then coaching a Major League eleven- and twelve-year-old game were miles apart. They were different, not only from the standpoint of skill, but in attention span and emotional maturity. It was very easy to make an eight-year-old cry or a twelve-year-old roll his eyes if you weren't paying attention to which game you were coaching.

There were advantages and disadvantages to coaching your own sons. One of the benefits was that the coach could take the bag of equipment home. The disadvantage was adequately summed up in the quote, "You can't be a prophet in your own land." At an older age, the tips I would give my boys started to fall on deaf ears. If, however, they received the exact same advice from another coach, they would follow it readily. I saw the same phenomenon later in my professional career. I would lay out a course of action for training my subordinates, and it would be met with polite smiles and basic indifference. If the same advice were given by a highly paid outside consultant, they couldn't wait to implement it. I am sure there is a logical explanation for this; I just haven't figured it out.

One of the most popular complaints parents have with coaches of youth sports is that they typically find ways to play their children over others. I was keenly aware of that and tried to be conscious of it. The challenge there was that Matt, Jimmy, and John were in the top 10 percent of the league in terms of skill and ability. They also learned not to be selfish or conceited, which made them all great team role models. A quick profile study of each of them here illustrates how different even brothers can be. When you coach or interact with any group of children at any age, these differences not only become painfully apparent but need to be recognized, understood, and nurtured.

Matt

Our eldest son always had a quiet confidence. He was a take-me-or-leave-me type of player who didn't tolerate a lot of practice and wasn't one to go out and do hitting drills on his own. He had perseverance and a consistency that was hard to find in young boys and teens. A testament to those traits was that in ten years of coaching baseball, he was one of only a few baseball players who went through the entire Oxford program, from eight-year-old T-ball to Senior Babe Ruth and high school, without missing a season.

Matt had an impressive last year in Little League and made the All-Star team. He really developed and matured in the Babe Ruth League. He was primarily an outfielder with great range and a knack for the ball. His inherent speed made him a great defensive threat and a great base runner.

Matt was also a quiet leader on the team. A good portion of the Babe Ruth team seemed to follow him like the Pied Piper through the thirteen-, fourteen-, and fifteen-year-old levels of the league.

Although he wasn't aggressive at the plate, he had surprising power. I remember a game that was played on the very field where I played my last game. Matt was batting with a runner on and connected on a high drive that was still going up as it cleared the right center-field fence. Fortunately for the cars parked on the other side of the fence, the ball also sailed over the parking lot and landed in the middle of the tennis courts. It was a monumental home run from someone who really never seemed to be aggressive on the field.

Matt also excelled at track and basketball. One day during one of his middle school track meets, I was sitting in the bleachers talking to some parents. I am embarrassed to say I wasn't really paying attention when the 4 × 200 relay started, but on the second leg, our runner seemed to explode from third place to first as they came around the far turn. I was doubly surprised to see that the runner at that point was Matt. That same relay team managed to set a school record that year.

Matt always enjoyed basketball when he wasn't playing baseball. He was, in fact, the primary motivation for starting the town basketball league for high school students. Again, it seemed that in the first year of the league, there was no trouble in finding enough players for our team, because his friends always seemed to rally around whatever he was doing.

Although he developed into a good three-point shooter, Matt always found other ways to contribute to the team's success. We were in a critical playoff game one year, and the game came down to the last minute, as we continued to exchange one-point leads with the opposition. At one point there was a scramble for the ball, which broke loose and was headed out of bounds by the midcourt scorers' table. Matt managed to chase the ball down and, just before crashing into the scorer's table, made an incredible behind-the-back pass to a teammate waiting under our basket, who banked in an uncontested layup to seal the game for us.

Matt's enthusiasm and love for sports certainly paved the way for his two younger brothers.

Jimmy

During his middle school and high school years, Jimmy assembled quite a portfolio of sporting interests, including baseball, Pop Warner Football, high school basketball, and cross country. Jimmy had a mix of tastes, talents, and personalities. From the time he could first start walking, he marched to his own drummer. He was always deceptively fast, with long loping strides that were hard for most to keep up with. Jimmy was a coach's player. He would play any position at any time or go bring the bases in and pack the bag after practice, with no exceptions and no back talk. In the time it took other players or to explain why they couldn't, Jimmy had it done.

Jimmy wasn't the most aggressive player on the field, and in his first year with the Minor League A's, he was so shy he went the better part of five games without swinging at a pitch. At one point, I considered bribing him just so he would swing the bat. He didn't have to make contact, just swing.

Jimmy gradually developed his own quiet confidence and was one of the few players I have coached who could consistently fill both the catcher's and pitcher's role on a team. Later, when I was coaching Jimmy in a Senior Babe Ruth League, we were in danger of forfeiting a game because we didn't have enough players. I had called the coach of our sister team and asked to borrow one of their players. In one of his absolutely useless responses, the coach reminded me that I had Jimmy. I said that although Jimmy was very talented and willing to play wherever he was asked to play, he could not pitch and catch at the same time. No, we never did get the extra player, and we had to forfeit the game.

As a counter to his laid-back, nonaggressive approach to sports, Jimmy announced his intention to play Pop Warner Football and did so for three seasons. He played offensive and defensive tackle. He was also the kicker and the punter.

Because of Jimmy's competitive nature, he wanted to play a bigger part in the offense, running the ball or catching passes. After he mentioned this a few time to us, my wife suggested I talk to his coach about this role change. One night after practice, I politely spoke with the coach with this new proposal of having Jimmy run the ball or catch passes. The coach responded by appealing to my own coaching experiences. "Look," he said, "Jimmy is one of the taller, bigger, more athletic players on the team; we need him on the offensive line. As a coach, I think this is where he can help the team the most."

I couldn't argue with that logic and reluctantly went back to report the decision to Beth. At the end of the next practice, she walked up to the coach and asked the same question. The coach responded with the same logical, polite explanation. When he was finished, Beth replied, "Yes, but why can't Jimmy run the ball?"

The coach recovered and restated his response from a different angle, still trying to make his point. When he was finished, Beth simply asked, "Yes, but why can't Jimmy run the ball?" The next game, Jimmy started at tight end and actually caught a touchdown pass. The lesson here is that sometimes, logic and good sense have no relevance in decision making.

Jimmy, like his brother Matt, was quite a leader with a great circle of friends. I would typically have three or four players on my teams that were there just because Jimmy was on the team. He was always a great influence on others.

John

From the time he first started walking, John was a rogue. My first revelation with John was in the front yard, just playing catch. He couldn't have been more than three or four years old at the time. I bought him a small glove that allowed him to catch with his left hand and throw with his right, like his brothers. One day, I threw the ball over his head, and as he chased it, he tossed his glove at the ball to stop it. By the time he reached the ball, he wasn't wearing a glove. He instinctively reached down with his left hand, picked up the ball, and fired it back at me with twice the speed and accuracy of his previous right-handed throws. I should have known things were going to be different from then on.

John was one of those rare athletes who had an innate talent for whatever game he played. At an early age, he learned to roller skate and announced he wanted to play roller hockey in the local league. Despite the fact he was a novice skater and knew next to nothing about hockey, he led the Junior League in scoring in his first year.

As a basketball player, he was one of the smallest players in the league. Despite his size, at eight years old he would shoot high, arcing twenty-foot shots that would cut clean through the nets. Parents and players alike would take two steps back in amazement, watching these bombs go through the net. John would punctuate these shots by running back down court on defense and doing an acrobatic somersault in the middle of the court on the way. In addition to baseball, he played soccer from sixth grade through high school, without ever attending a soccer camp or playing on a premier team. He frequently led his teams in scoring and completed his high school soccer career by scoring two goals in the championship game. He was voted Most Valuable Player. John always seemed to have a sense of where to be at the right time.

Matt was a right-handed batter and right-handed thrower, Jimmy was a left-handed batter and right-handed thrower, and John was a left-handed batter and left-handed thrower. That alone summarized for me how different brothers can be and how much good coaching is dependent on recognizing those differences and making them work for you. Although they are just a very small and insignificant dot on the map of young athletes worldwide, they do represent a cross section of every coach's challenge. Even three brothers can be remarkably different in skills, desire, and temperament. As a coach and certainly as a father, my success had a lot to do with recognizing these differences and looking to leverage and maximizing them.

The Majors

Coaching in the eleven- and twelve-year-old Little League division brought new challenges. As the players grew older, the teams became more competitive. If a player made it this far in the program, they weren't just trying out a new activity; they had expressed an interest and an aptitude as a player. This was the first level where I could really concentrate on refining the skills of players. It was also the first level where I could begin to talk about and execute game strategy.

There was a balance that needed to be reached between developing a team and developing individual players. My first year as an assistant in this division, I coached with Jeff, who had a twelve-year-old son on the team. Jeff alternated between his son and another twelve-year-old for constant pitching duties for the team that year.

Although we had a good year and both twelve-year-old pitchers made the All-Star team, we had no reserves and certainly no pitching prospects for the following year. Since Jeff and his son graduated after that year, I was left with a promotion to head coach and no pitching prospects.

If you coach for more than one year with the same team, you can almost be assured of a new crop of players coming in the next year. For us, about half the team were new players from the previous year's eight- through ten-year-old program.

There were other requirements of a Major League coach. We had to take first aid and a basic coach's workshop. We installed a batting cage and acquired a pitching machine. The batting cage drill was one more thing to schedule as a separate practice. Practices became tougher to manage logistically at this level. It was more important to break practices down into infield and outfield drills, batting practice, and pitching drills. It required more coaches and interested parents. As practices and games became more involved, it seemed that my assistant coaching reserves became less and less. Other parents with boys on the team were content to sit in the bleachers during practice and read the paper (or worse yet, drop them off and leave).

There are times as a coach when you walk a fine line between trying to develop skill and confidence in a game, and creating emotional turmoil. Early in one of the seasons as a head coach, I had used Jimmy as a starting pitcher. I had not tested anyone else to this point, and it was clearly a case of "the devil you know versus the devil you don't know."

The game started off on rocky footing. The Phillies scored three runs off us in the first inning, and Jimmy was noticeably upset on the pitcher's mound. I called timeout and walked out to the mound to talk to him.

"Dad, get me out of here," he said, "I can't pitch."

"Jimmy," I said, "we have no one else we can use right now, I just want you to take a breath and make believe it's practice and just throw."

He looked at me with those tearful beagle eyes and said, "Okay, Dad."

Jimmy managed to get the next batter out and then proceeded to pitch five scoreless innings, striking out eleven batters. We won the game, 5–3. That is not an example of good coaching; it is a matter of character and perseverance. Yes, it was a miraculous display of a comeback with almost flawless pitching, but that's not the story. The real story is that he wiped away the tears and gave it everything he had for as long as we needed him. If he let in six more runs, it still would have been a truly brave performance by an eleven-year-old.

I gradually learned to assess talent on the team fairly quickly. On the one hand, I needed to get a handle on the best hitters, pitchers, throwers, and catchers. I needed to place strengths in the positions I thought might do us the most good. At the same time, I was looking to manage weaknesses. I needed to provide some opportunities for certain players to develop skills and take on new responsibilities while making sure they were still having fun.

As we continued to advance through the system into next level leagues, I started to see the leagues get somewhat diluted. This dilution was not only apparent in individual baseball skills but also in overall enthusiasm for the game. Soccer was becoming a more popular sport for elementary school children, and many were gravitating toward that and other activities. By the time my two older sons had graduated to the Babe Ruth level, the ranks of the eleven- and twelve-year-olds were getting thin. This was getting to be such a problem that the eleven- and twelve-year-old league was looking for reasonably talented prospects to be brought up from the eight- to ten-year-old level.

John was one of those promising Minor Leaguers being considered. He was small for his age, and although considered a ten-year-old, he was still a month shy of his tenth birthday when he was called up to the Pirates.

John was truly a sapling among the redwoods, and it was funny to watch him stand in at the plate. Although getting used to Major League pitching was an obvious obstacle for John, he did have two significant offensive weapons. The first was that he had the family genes for speed. He was fast on the base paths and on defense. The second was that because of his size, he had almost no strike zone. Trying to throw the ball over the plate between John's letters and his knees was like trying to throw a tennis ball through the mouth of a cardboard cutout clown at the carnival.

I was asked to coach this Major League team as part of the trade deal, realizing that the coaching population was dwindling at the same speed as the player population. After a few days of assessing my new team, I came to the conclusion that the talent ranks on the team were thinner than I had anticipated, and I needed to get creative.

I only had three legitimate hitters at the time, out of a lineup of nine players. My strategy was to have John be leadoff hitter and then evenly disperse the other three dependable hitters at the third, fifth, and seventh spots in the lineup. There were pros and cons to this plan, but it seemed to be the best solution at the time.

Batting first, John almost guaranteed us a leadoff base runner as long as he didn't swing at any balls over his head. He was also usually good for at least one stolen base or moving up a base on a wild pitch or a passed ball. Hopefully we would get some sort of production out of the second batter in the order, and then I would have one of my best hitters following.

Because of the mix of talent on our team, and certainly on the teams we faced, it created a variety of ever-changing situations. One of the managerial skills that I became very good at was in giving signs to the batters and base runners. There were three basic tasks that need to be communicated to players during the course of a game. Shouting out these instructions to your players was a dead giveaway to the other team. Therefore, there were basic signs that were developed to communicate the instructions. These were the three tasks:

1. Bunt: Tapping the ball with your bat to move the base runner along. This usually is called a sacrifice bunt because you are almost assured of being an out in exchange for moving the runner up into scoring position.

2. Take: Actually means don't swing at the next pitch; let it go by no matter what.

3. Hit: Free to swing away and hit the ball, providing you get a good pitch to hit.

To communicate these directions during a game, we needed to attach a sign to each one of these functions. Usually the signs are some visible body part that the player can see from the field. These signs always change from game to game.

Let's say, as an example, I wanted my batter to bunt the ball in a particular situation. While giving the pregame batting order and positions, we also go over the signs as a team. Everyone understands that when I touch my elbow, it means to bunt the next pitch. Things get a little more complicated at this point. You don't have to be a secret agent to break that code after the first time it is used. If I touch my elbow, and only my elbow, and the batter bunts the next pitch, anyone still awake on the opposing team will know that the next time I touch my elbow, the batter is going to bunt. Therefore, I need to embed touching my elbow in the middle of some other meaningless signs.

Now you may ask, "How do I know which is the right sign to use?" Great question! The set of signs also includes an indicator sign; all the other signs are dummy signs. The real sign is the very next sign after the indicator sign. For example, let us assume that the indicator sign is touching my nose. If I want the batter to bunt and the bunt sign is touching my elbow, the series of signs might look like this:

Touch cap	Dummy
Touch shoulder	Dummy
Touch elbow	Dummy
Touch nose	Indicator
Touch elbow	Sign
Touch wrist	Dummy
Touch cap	Dummy

Notice that I didn't end the sequence with the actual sign, because that would also be a giveaway. The fact that I touched my elbow early on meant nothing, because it didn't follow the indicator sign (touching my nose). Only when I touched my elbow immediately after touching my nose did the sign have any meaning.

As the season progressed, I was able to refine and expand the sign system to cover other situations. John became so skilled at stealing bases that I created a special sign for him when I wanted him to steal. I would look at the batter and just hitch up my belt. That hitching had no meaning to the batter at the plate, but John would know to steal on the very next pitch. Some of the players on our team became skilled at receiving signs, and I even had an opportunity to teach them how to give signs. Other players had no clue, and I might as well have been trying to teach them the Sumerian cuneiform alphabet.

The Scorebook

Another Major League coaching responsibility was keeping the scorebook. The scorebook was more than just a list of players, the batting order, and their positions. It was also a reminder that there were nine positions and usually twelve or thirteen players on the team; everyone had to play at least two innings during the game. Anytime that requirement wasn't met, you were sure to be reminded by an irate parent that they had not paid good money just to watch their junior star sit on the bench.

The scorebook also emphasized the need that, as a coach, your head had to be in two places at once. The first was in what was going on in the game at that point in time. What was happening on the next pitch? The other was that even as early as the first inning, you needed to be looking ahead to the fourth, fifth, and sixth inning and plan for who was going to do what, who had played, who hadn't played, where should they play, who should sit down, and what if we need another pitcher?

Most of the time, with all this activity and decision making on their plate, coaches realized that they were performing all these activities before the watchful and critical eyes of parents, most of whom thought they could do it better but had no intention of helping. Well, I take that back; I have had the pleasure of knowing parents who willingly participated in everything from assistant coach to team mom, helping to make phone calls and collect money for pictures and other fundraising novelties.

Little League coaches not only had to be fluent in the rules and strategies of the game, they also needed to be statisticians, administrative assistants, nurses, and in some cases disciplinarians for all the event and possibilities that go on during practice and games. These duties were multiplied exponentially if, like me, you were coaching two teams (one year, I coached three teams at once). During one season, I coached both the Minor League Marlins and the Major League Marlins. Multitasking through the course of a normal workday, I was notified that our game that evening was going to be canceled. I proceeded to call all the players and parents to notify them of the change in schedule. I no sooner hung up from the tenth of twelve of these last-minute phone calls when I realized I called the wrong Marlins team. Needless to say, I spent a lot of time on the phone that night.

In some rare cases, the coach had to take on the role of surrogate parent. I was surprised at the number of young Little Leaguers who came from divorced or single parents. Some parents wouldn't or couldn't stay for the game. It would hurt to look at their faces in the dugout, straining to see if there was anyone in the bleachers that they knew, if there was a father or mother or someone that would shout out their name as they walked up to the plate to take their turn at bat. There were times where you knew there wasn't anyone there. I tried to reserve some extra attention for them. I would give them special jobs to help me during a game and try to give them additional encouragement and praise when it was their turn in the spotlight. There were nights where we would finish a game or a practice and I would sit with a single player in the bleachers, just the two of us, waiting for a parent or guardian to pick them up. I would go home and have dinner that night and say a little prayer, giving thanks that I had the opportunity to be in the dugout with my sons.

Golden Moments

There were very memorable incidents, good and bad, in those years I spent coaching and watching Little League games. There were times when the most unlikely of players made some of the most miraculous plays. One summer evening, we were in a tight game with the league-leading Phillies, who managed to load the bases with two outs and one of their best hitters coming up. I looked around the outfield and saw Anthony squinting into home plate; the summer sun was setting behind the backstop, and he was looking right into it. Anthony was a great kid with a positive attitude, but he wasn't very mobile.

As luck would have it, the Phillies batter connected on the next pitch and hit a screaming line drive to, of all places, left field. I jumped out from behind the protective screen in the dugout, and my first thought was that this would clear the bases, scoring two, three, maybe even four runs with one swing of the bat. The ball headed right for Anthony and I held my breath. As the ball closed in on Anthony's position, he just raised his left arm head-high and the ball hit his glove. A game-saving catch and he never took a step, not that he could have. If that ball had gotten past Anthony, it would have been Tuesday before he finally caught up with it. It truly was one of the league's most memorable moments.

There were other moments that I wasn't particularly proud of. As a coach, you try to teach the kids how to play the game, how to work together as a team, and to always display good sportsmanship. We are all human, though, and sometimes even the best of us loses it in certain circumstances.

Later in my Little League coaching experience, the league had instituted a rule that we could use some teenaged players from the Babe Ruth League as umpires. They had to go through an orientation, but otherwise they were ready to go, and we had a few interested prospects.

One such game we had two of these young umpires, one behind the plate calling balls and strikes and one positioned at first base. During one inning, one of our players became trapped in a rundown between third base and home. The catcher and third baseman ran our player back and forth between third and home in a play that must have lasted at least thirty to forty-five seconds. Finally, after he dove back into third base, our runner was called out by the first-base umpire. I lost it! I came storming out of the dugout and headed toward the first-base umpire. In the ensuing verbal exchange, I finally said to the wide-eyed teen, "I am not arguing because you called him out. I am arguing because you called him out from all the way over by first base, while the play happened at third. The play took so long to be completed that you had plenty of time to walk, if not run, all the way across the field to stand three feet away from the play when you finally made the call!" Judging by the wide-eyed look on the teen's face, I realized that my outburst did more harm than good. In a quieter postgame moment, I walked out with him and used it as a teaching opportunity. He admitted that my point, in a normal conversational tone, made sense.

As my two older sons moved on to the Babe Ruth League and my youngest son was finishing up his last year in Little League, I could start to feel the final curtain coming down on my coaching experience. In many ways, coaching not only gave me a chance to give back and share some of the wonderful memories I had with Little League baseball, but it selfishly allowed me one more day on the field. This bittersweet time was tempered with the gradual dilution and manipulation that continued to go on in most leagues. Coaches were subtly influencing player selection, schedules, and even some rules to benefit themselves and their teams. Parents were complaining about All-Star team selection and playing time for their children. I desperately wanted to stay, and I desperately wanted to go.

I also found that as some of the players grew older, they had more commitments, including the growing popularity of soccer, which started to split their allegiance and commitment. Being as dedicated as I was to baseball, I found it a little annoying that I would keep losing players to a game that wasn't even an American sport, let alone our national pastime.

Ironically, about the time John was finishing his Little League career, he began playing soccer for his middle school. In the years that followed, he became (with no formal training) one of the most prolific soccer and track performers in the area. In high school, John was All State in both sports and led his high school soccer team to the league championship, scoring a remarkable thirty-four goals in two seasons. Since I knew next to nothing about soccer, I was never in a position to coach, especially at that level. With John marching to a different drummer, my waning coaching days were focused on both levels of the Babe Ruth League.

Babe Ruth Would Roll Over in His Grave

Just as I had to make a transition from T-ball to Little League, so too did I have to take the next leap into the Babe Ruth League. Babe Ruth, or as we referred to it back in the Stone Ages, Pony League, was for Little League graduates, boys from thirteen to fifteen years old. There was also a senior division for boys sixteen to eighteen years old. These levels started to weed out the players who were truly interested in baseball from those who were just looking for another activity for the summer.

The division between twelve-year-old Little Leaguers and thirteen-year-old Babe Ruth players was probably the greatest gap to fill in my experience as a coach of youth baseball. For a start, the field itself was of regulation size. This meant that the distance between the bases was ninety feet instead of Little League's sixty-foot-long base paths. The distance from the pitcher's mound to home plate was longer, and the distance between home plate and second base was also longer, making it harder for a catcher to throw out a base stealer.

Another critical challenge in this league was the fact that the difference between a player just turning thirteen years old and one who is almost seventeen could be like David and Goliath. The logical thing to do would be to have the thirteen-year-olds play in a league of their own and group the fourteen- and fifteen-year-olds in a separate league. However, good sense and significantly decreasing enrollments caused us to ignore logic and group them all together. Some thirteen-year-old boys who were not as aggressive as some of their sixteen-year-old counterparts spent most of the year playing minimally and striking out almost every time they came to bat. Since no one was getting paid for the games and we were playing for fun and enjoyment, the fun was rapidly disappearing. Sadly, some of these baseball hopefuls quit halfway through the season out of frustration.

Just when you thought this was a big enough hill to climb in promoting the program, we also had a third major obstacle. The Babe Ruth League expanded beyond the borders of our hometown and included neighboring towns. That meant that these game were against teams and players we didn't know. Most of these programs were larger and more sophisticated than our program, and it showed on the field.

A glitch in our hometown baseball program was that not enough time was spent on outfield strategy. The outfield was where they put the younger players in the league. The thought was you had the older players in front of them in the infield and the fence was behind them in the outfield. How much trouble could they get into? This attitude didn't do much to develop experienced older outfielders.

I was reunited with my oldest son Matt again as his coach in the Senior Babe Ruth division. Most of these players at the sixteen- to eighteen-year-old level were big and experienced (some of them were bigger than I was). They were not only more physically capable but certainly more in need of a detailed baseball strategy. The idea of moving the defense around based on a batter's past performance was new to our program. The strategy of pitch selection, for both pitchers and batters, needed to be refined. The teams we were playing were more sophisticated and knew how to make the mental part of the game work for them.

We tried to work on some of these skills early in our preseason practices while trying to slot the players we had into the most logical positions for their talents. Most of our players had come up through the ranks, others had joined later on, and some even started their baseball experience with Babe Ruth League.

I will never forget opening day of my last year as coach of the sixteen- to eighteen-year-old Babe Ruth team. It was a beautiful late spring day, and the field was in great condition. I was just finishing the lineup in the book, looked down the bench, and saw Matt standing at the bat rack. His new pinstripe uniform was spotless in the pregame sun. I remember thinking back to his first day in T-ball as an eight-year-old, ten years earlier. What an incredible man he had become, while using his passion and determination to complete this incredible journey to the end of the program. No matter how we fared in this last year, I realized what a privilege it was to share this experience with him.

The Orioles

My coaching responsibilities were now confined to just two teams, the seniors and the thirteen-year-old team. This was a transitional team but one that we could work with because everyone on the team, and everyone in this league, was basically the same age.

The Orioles were a collection of the previous twelve-year-old graduates from our Little League program. We had a fairly stable roster, and Tom Peters, one of the fathers, volunteered to be the assistant coach. Tom wasn't exactly an encyclopedia of baseball knowledge, but in a sea of ever-increasing apathy and lack of commitment, he was a welcome addition.

We managed to put together a respectable year, and although we weren't going to win any championships, I was committed to having some fun and exploring the limits with the team. I tried mixing up positions, giving players new experiences. We were also more aggressive in our play selections and on the base paths. We used the steal and the double steal and the suicide squeeze bunt in low percentage situations, often catching the other team off guard.

I found ways to instill a little fire in the team once in a while when we started to get a little sluggish. One game in particular, we were behind and really had nothing going on offensively.

Anthony was at the plate, the player who made the game-saving catch against Phillies. After fouling off repeated pitches, Anthony was called out on a highly doubtful third strike. As he left home plate to walk back to the dugout, the umpire gave him an emphatic ejection signal, throwing him out of the game. Apparently he thought he had heard Anthony make some comment or derogatory remark.

Now before I share with you what happened next, you need to know that Anthony was about as soft spoken and mild mannered a young man as God has ever put on this planet. I had never seen him get upset or raise his voice in the four years I had known him. When the umpire ejected him from the game, I saw red! I raced down from my third-base coach's box straight at the home-plate umpire like a linebacker chasing a quarterback. I stopped inches from his face and proceeded to scream at him in a rage, which he was not prepared for. When I was finished unloading in this one-way conversation, I took a deep breath and turned to the head umpire, who had waddled down from his first-base position to help out. I looked at the head umpire, pointed to the home-plate umpire, and screamed, "If you ever show up to one of our games with him again, I will take my team off the field and you won't get paid!" The game continued and my tirade was like blowing a bugle for sleeping soldiers. We scored more runs in the last two innings than we did in the previous five.

Yes, there were frustrating times and disappointments as a coach, but there were so many happy and satisfying experiences and events that it is hard to name them all. Some were celebrated as a team and some were quiet moments in a young boy's life where you hoped you made a difference. The experience of participating, enjoying, and benefiting from sports has always been like an iceberg to me. The games, the home runs, the baskets, and the goals were great and memorable, but they were just the tip of the iceberg. It was the human interaction, building confidence, and the bonding under a single purpose that was the lasting part. I have forgotten the scores of many games, but I will never forget the look on the one boy's face on my team. His parents could never find the time to attend his games. He would sneak a peek into the bleachers during the game, hoping against hope that one of them would be there, yelling his name. He became a friend who sat with me side-by-side, helping me keep score. He was my assistant in the dugout, my helper who would walk me to my car, trying to squeeze one last minute out of an evening he didn't want to end. That was coaching!

Knocked Off My Feet

There were also moments that literally knocked me off my feet. I was coaching a Senior Babe Ruth League game one night at our home field. The game was just beginning against our neighbor team in the next town. The pitcher was finishing his pregame warm-up tosses, and I had walked out to home plate to meet the opposing coach and umpires. As we began to exchange lineup cards, I suddenly felt a stinging pain in my face and then everything went black. When I opened my eyes a short time later, I was staring up into a crowd of faces, everyone asking me if I was okay. I saw the flashing red lights from emergency vehicles and felt myself being lifted up off the ground. I was conscious enough to realize I was being loaded into a waiting ambulance. Later, I was told that one of the last warm-up pitches from the big seventeen-year-old righthander sailed over his catcher's head and hit me square in the cheek, somewhere between my lip and my eye. An inch or two in either direction, and I could have lost an eye (or all my teeth).

The ironic thing about this story is that I pleaded with Matt not to call his mother for about an hour or so until I was checked out at the hospital. I knew Beth was at my youngest son's soccer game, and I didn't want her to leave knowing that John would be looking up into the bleachers. Yes, Beth did see John's entire soccer game, and yes, I was severely reprimanded for exhibiting poor decision making.

The further we moved into the season, the more things continued to erode. Life was no different at the Senior Babe Ruth level. We had a midseason game scheduled with the senior team from Meriden, Connecticut, a good forty-five-minute drive from our town. Fortunately for us, it was a home game, and I arrived at the field early to finish some groundskeeping in preparation for our out-of-town guests. About forty minutes before game time, the Meriden team started pulling in, most of the cars driven by the teenage players. They had perfect attendance, and after their coach and I introduced ourselves, we began the formality of exchanging lineup cards and going over the ground rules. While the preliminary warm-ups were progressing, I couldn't help noticing a group of local men assembling on the softball field, which was in straightaway center field of our field.

I ran over and asked what they were doing. One of these middle-aged weekend warriors informed me they had a regularly scheduled softball game about to take place as part of the men's weekend recreational league. I let them know that we had a game scheduled with an out-of-town travel team, and because our game was baseball and not softball, we had to use this field. In the middle of the ensuing argument, our director of parks and recreation managed to make a personal appearance. We were informed that the men's game had been scheduled first, and if our league director was more efficient in his scheduling, we could have kept our field. As it stood, the men's softball game was on and our game was off. Once again, petty politics won out, and our hometown teens had to sacrifice. At least those twenty-four grown men had their precious two hours of playtime.

There is nothing I can say to describe to you the embarrassment I felt that day, having to go back to that coach and tell his team the game was off. I walked back slowly to tell them that their forty-minute drive was for nothing. There would be no game.

After that season, coaching baseball started to break up for a variety of very good reasons. Matt finished his last season and received his jacket for completing the entire program. Jim had gone on to high school baseball, track, and basketball, which replaced his Babe Ruth experience. The fragment of the town league that was left was really a showcase for the few coaches' sons and their buddies. All the wonderful memories of playing and coaching, the experience of being side by side with each of my sons, was coming to a logical and timely conclusion. The Fourth of July fireworks were finally fizzling into the last sparks and smoke of an amazing time of life.

These are the days that we'll remember

These are the days that won't come again,

The highest of flames becomes an ember

You better live them while you can.

—*Keith Urban*

Oxford Youth Basketball

The evolutionary process of coaching youth baseball was made an even more extraordinary experience for me given the fact that I had an almost identical experience with youth basketball as I did with baseball. I had the same three sons and the same three age groups going through the same experiences trials and tribulations. The only major differences were that there was no bat and the ball was bigger.

At the time my sons entered the basketball program, there was only a junior and senior league. These leagues were comparable to the Minor and Major Little League age groups. All three of my sons expressed more than a little interest in playing basketball, and so I conducted my research and we were enrolled. Again, my development as a coach started with being an avid parent supporter in the stands with Matt in his first season as a junior. Gradually, I worked my way from the upper bleachers to the lower bleachers to sitting behind the bench. From there I could be an extra pair of hands for anything from retrieving balls after warm-up drills to passing out schedules. It was only a matter of time that with my enthusiasm, coupled with my sad, beagle-like eyes, I would get my chance.

Jim Chernesky

Junior Basketball Assistant to Head Coach

As an assistant junior basketball coach, I tried early on to keep my eyes and ears open, to watch the head coach and the other coaches to see what gems of knowledge I could collect. I realized that with three young sons, my involvement in this sport would only grow deeper and more intense. Basketball, however, was a sport that I knew less about in terms of skill and strategy compared to baseball, and it was certainly a sport in which I was much less adept. I had smaller hands, I was not that tall, and I was never really taught the proper way to shoot. Because my hands were so small, I relied on two-handed shooting, which went out of style a long time ago.

Since I was coming from a little further back in the pack on this sport, I spent more time studying, listening to other experts, and again trying to find ways to transfer knowledge and skills to a level where it could be effective yet fun.

It didn't take long to realize, as in most sports and youth activities like Cub Scouts, that things flow along fairly well and are fun until adults get involved. I have had the pleasure of working with some great youth coaches who never had a son or daughter in the league at the time. They coached for the fun and passion of the game and obviously at least a little desire to give back. Most coaches, however, did have a child or three that was playing. Quite naturally, these coaches often went out of their way to provide a winning environment for their own child prodigy, who almost always was placed on their father's or mother's team.

I know, I know, this is far from the norm in children's leagues. There are good people, great coaches, and supportive parents. The competitive nature of sports, however, even at early ages, combined with self-serving coaches and unreasonable and often belligerent parents, makes for a flammable combination.

One such ugly display of this phenomenon happened toward the end Jimmy's last year in junior basketball. By then, through the natural purging of the coaching ranks and the indifference of most other new parents to ever get involved, I had worked my way to the head coach position. We were competing in a playoff series toward the end of the season. As luck would have it, we were playing a particularly competitive, "stop-at-nothing" team of ten- and eleven-year-olds with a coach who reinforced all of those endearing qualities.

The teams in this league had nine or ten players on the roster, which evolved throughout the league into an A and a B team. The A team obviously was composed of the best five players on the team, and the B players were, well, let's say not as skilled as the A team. There was an unwritten rule that when coaches substituted players for equal playing time, they substituted the As and Bs at the same time. This theoretically eliminated obvious physical and skill mismatches during the game. The other interesting variable in all this was that the league was coed. That's right, girls and boys together. Now you should know that the league made every attempt to distribute girls evenly throughout the teams. You also have to guess who usually managed to have the most girls on his team in any given season . . . That's right, ole Coach "He won't mind, he loves kids" Jim.

Let's go back to the playoff game in question. I had a set of twin brothers who played on this team, the older, Robert, being bigger and taller but somewhat learning disabled, which made him slower and less coordinated than his brother. After careful analysis during the season, I placed the smaller brother of the two on the A team and his bigger, more physically challenged brother on the B team.

Well, as in any Hollywood script, the game was a nail-biting, too-close-to-call contest that went back and forth the entire game. As we started the last quarter, the opposing coach stomped over to where I was standing, smoke and fire streaming from his nostrils similar to Yosemite Sam in the Warner Bothers cartoons. In a voice that everyone in the bleachers could plainly hear, he accused me of using one of my A players, the bigger brother on the B team, to gain an unfair advantage. I quietly tried to explain the differences between the two brothers in a voice that would not embarrass the less skilled brother, who was sitting a few feet away. The coach, however, would have none of the explanation and threatened to protest the game. I guess he felt his multimillion-dollar contract with the public school system and his appearance on ESPN, not to mention the trip to Disneyland after he had won the game, were all in jeopardy.

During the fourth quarter, a period that according to Hollywood script rules was going to be played by the two A teams, the tension mounted considerably. The stage was set for a fight to the death, and because of the loud and boisterous coach, everyone in the gym knew what was at stake. What followed were eight of the proudest minutes I ever had as a coach for youth sports. Leaving only Jimmy in for the whole period (he was the tallest on the team, but not by much), I freely substituted B players for A players every two minutes throughout the entire last period. Naturally, the other team left their A players in for the entire period. The only instructions I gave my team was to play harder than they have ever played before. We managed to play them evenly thought the first six minutes. Jimmy, only eleven years old, seemed to be playing in his own world, having fun and making point after point, completely oblivious of the ugliness going on around him.

As we entered the final two minutes, I glanced up into our parents' cheering section and saw faces of happiness and disbelief that four-foot-tall Mary would be playing in the final two minutes of a competitive free-for-all that apparently meant so much. It also became obvious that the only way the opposition was going to win this game was to stop Jimmy's seemingly oblivious, cool-handed, almost flawless performance. The opposing team started fouling him every time he touched the ball in the last minute of play. He would calmly step to the foul line and make both shots as though he were playing a video game in his own room. The opposition would then race frantically down the court, letting their best player take the next shot with many of our B players in hot pursuit. Two more fouls shots from Jimmy, and one more frantic attempt at the buzzer, and we walked away with a hard-earned two-point victory.

At the conclusion of the game, after all the required well wishes and handshaking, the opposing coach walked over to me with congratulations. He shook my hand, apologized for his outburst, and said that we had played a good and fair game.

There is no way to tell this story without making it sound like "hurray for me," but that's not what this is about. It is an example of the best and the worst of sports. I saw one of the fathers of a B team player twelve years after that game. He wanted to tell me how much it meant to his son's self-esteem and confidence to play in the last period of that game. The incredible truth about his comment had nothing to do with the fact that we won the game. It would have been just as true if we lost by two, ten, or twenty points.

Expanding the League; the Automated Schedule

During my first year of coaching the Junior League (ages nine through eleven), I became more familiar with the administrative side of coaching: uniforms, practices, schedules, and makeup games. Oh yes, and occasionally dealing with parents. To round out this league, we also had a Senior League (ages twelve and thirteen). Each league had six teams, and we played games at different schools in town. We scheduled weeknight games and practices from six to nine o'clock during the week and from nine o'clock to noon on Saturdays. Armed with this list of teams, times, and locations, a group of coach volunteers would assemble at a select coach's house one evening after work and proceed to create a schedule for both leagues from December through March.

The scheduling process was a veritable Rubik's cube with almost no logical solution. Not only were we manipulating dates and locations and trying to arrange it so that all teams play each other in different locations, but we would also have to factor in school calendars, holidays, snow days, and so on. If that wasn't enough, every coach in this session had a hidden agenda. The underlying politics of this little exercise was enough to start a brand-new soap opera.

We had limped through this exercise and managed to put a paper schedule together that moved us through my first year of coaching. They say, "Time flies when you're having fun," and before long it was the beginning of my second season as a coach. Again we were faced with this almost impossible schedule. Agonizing over our impending scheduling meeting coming up, my mind started to wander. Major League Baseball was comprised of twenty-plus teams, twenty-plus locations all over the United States. Each team plays 162 games between May 1 and September 30. We had half a dozen volunteer coaches sitting around a kitchen table, moving little team squares around. There had to be a better way.

There was! I had completed some Internet research (1997 Internet research, so we aren't really talking Google or Windows 7 here) and found a company that sold school scheduling software. I believe at the time it was twenty-nine dollars and came on a three-inch floppy diskette. No Windows, no self-loading icons, no drop-down menus, but it did allow you to put all the information in, each individual team, dates and times available, locations available, holidays and dates to avoid. My hands were shaking as I anticipated what was about to happen.

I pushed Enter on my computer, and no fewer than thirty sheets of paper came spitting out of my printer. I was afraid to look. When I did, I couldn't believe what I saw.

Individual schedules for each of the junior and senior teams were neatly printed. There was also a master schedule and a statistics page, including standings. As games were played, scores could be entered and the software would print standings and individual team statistics. It was absolutely amazing! We could also do some "what if" scheduling. We could start the schedule on October 9 and then rerun the whole schedule starting on October 16 with the push of a button. The schedule was not only accurate but free of personal agendas and politics.

Within the next year, we were able to expand the league from junior and senior boys to include a junior and senior girls' league, a Biddy League (ages seven to eight), and eventually a High School League (coed). The league grew by roughly 300 percent. Although the scheduling was still not without its imperfections, we all agreed there were many more pluses than minuses, and we worked to refine our new system.

On the Board

The basketball scheduling software was truly one of my biggest personal contributions to youth sports in the town. There is an old saying, "No good deed shall go unpunished," and that was certainly true in this case. At our next coach's meeting, I was promptly elected to the Youth Basketball Board of Directors.

By this time, I had a son in the Senior League and one in the Junior League. I was head coach of both teams, which meant two different practices, two sets of games, and two sets of "never happy" parents. The additional responsibility of board membership required periodic meetings where our group of directors would make executive decisions on everything from playoff schedules to uniform colors. Occasionally we also had our typical human resources issues involving delinquent players and irate coaches.

Jim Chernesky

A Walk through Your Favorite Restaurant

Making the transition from interested parent spectator to helper, assistant coach, coach, league director, and board member happened relatively quickly. It was also an experience that exposed the inner workings and the behind-the-scenes logistics and politics that hid under the surface. As an illustration of this phenomenon, let me present the following analogy.

Picture your favorite restaurant (not a diner or a fast food place). See yourself walking up to the restaurant, ready to open the front door. You are met with some impressive outdoor ambiance. The scene includes beautiful lighting and manicured grounds, possibly with flowers and other adornments. You see the external richness of the architecture, topped off by an inviting front door. You go inside to the warm smile of the hostess, subdued lighting, white tablecloths, and red linen. After you look over the menu, you go to the rear of the restaurant to use the restroom. As you walk by the kitchen door, it swings open and for a moment you catch a glimpse of the inner workings. People dressed in food-stained white uniforms hustling about and yelling out orders and, in some cases, excuses. You can hear the clash of dirty dishes and steam coming from stoves and grills. All the way in the back is a hall with a door to the loading dock, a dark and dirty area where trucks and delivery personnel slide in and out. Rusted dock rails, beat-up Dumpsters, some graffiti, and a mouse or two running across the wooden stairs that lead out the door top off this restaurant experience.

For me, the journey through the youth basketball organizational chart from interested parent to board member was very much like walking through that restaurant. The more involved I became, and the more responsibility I accepted, the more I was privy to the dirty inner workings of the parent-led, politically motivated inner workings of the leagues. I also realized that there are well-meaning, unselfish parents who, in addition to their personal lives, families, and full-time jobs, take on these responsibilities because so many enthusiastic kids are standing at the front door of the restaurant, waiting to get in. Most of the time, these dedicated individuals shoulder this mountain of responsibility on a volunteer basis and with more criticism than thanks. Criticism came from others who could barely scrape together enough time to drive their young sports enthusiast to a game, let alone be there for support.

Now before you jump on me for that last statement, I already know what they would say. "Hey, bud, I do what I can, I have a long commute. I leave at five o'clock in the morning and get back at eight o'clock at night. I barely have time to eat and kiss my spouse before getting up to do it all over again." Believe me, I know that and understand it. I think that's why all of us, in our own way, need to find a middle ground of involvement and bonding with those we love.

I was blessed with the opportunity to work for the same company for fifteen years, which was located fifteen minutes from my home. With almost no overnight travel, I was home every night and could make extensive commitments to coaching and organizing and running events and activities that my sons were involved in. I had a real chance to be an active part of their lives and took advantage of it. I was even a scout leader and, for one Christmas pack meeting, even Santa Claus! At the time I accepted that job, I had an opportunity to be hired by a prestigious organization in Manhattan. Truth be told, there were two undeniable truths to that crossroads in my life. The first was that the position in New York was much more visible and lucrative than the one fifteen minutes from home would ever be. If I had taken that position, I would have been one of those people with the "I leave at five o'clock in the morning and get back at eight o'clock at night" syndrome. The second truth here is that if I had had the choice between both at the time, I would have taken the position in New York, hands down. As it was, through a series of obstacles and corporate red tape, the New York position was delayed, and because I needed a paycheck, I accepted the local position.

For me, there are no words, no amount of money, to compare the richness and joy for my wife and me being home every night to literally watch our boys grow up and participate in life. It was very rewarding for us as parents knowing that every time the boys looked up, we were both in the bleachers, if not on the bench.

The experience as a member of the board did present opportunities to do more than just provide some competitive recreation to our children. Membership provided a chance to do what I was really looking to do all along, and that was to share some of the good feelings and experiences I had participating in sports as a boy with future generations.

One of those administrative challenges involved the league referees. Each season, prior to the start, while we were still mulling over schedules and colors for uniforms, we went through the process of recruiting, training, and scheduling referees to officiate all the games. Now let me preface all this by saying that the job of basketball referee, baseball umpire, or football official is a dirty, thankless job in itself. Think about it: No matter how good you are, no matter how keen your eyesight, or how much previous experience you have, you are guaranteed to make enemies of 50 percent of the people watching your performance every time you make a call. It's bad enough when the call goes against your favorite sports figure on the televised game of the week. You can always curse and throw a hot wing at the big screen. When it happens at a live event and the call goes against your own flesh and blood, things can get truly ugly.

As a league director, I came up with an idea for officials to use in a game, especially for the younger players. We asked all the referees during their training and orientation to make the call and then briefly explain what the player did wrong and how to avoid it next time. If they turned it into a mini teaching moment, they not only reinforced their reason for the call, they also presented it on a positive note to the perpetrator, giving them a quick tip on how to avoid the infraction in the future. The arguments and value judgments from the bleachers still occurred, but they were shorter, less threatening, and more easily defended.

Another innovation that we started with the referees was that in addition to the few certified referees we had, we also tapped into our teen crowd, who at this point did not have a formal high school recreational league to play in. I was surprised at the number of older siblings who took advantage of this opportunity. We even purchased striped shirts and whistles for them. As potentially great an idea as this seemed to be, it did have its downside. When a bad call did come up, the spectators had a new argument at their fingertips. "How could we let kids referee kids?" I have to say that back in my days of playing basketball at twelve years old, we managed very nicely to officiate our own games without the help of adults. Again, I probably missed the memo on this.

Another weak link in this chain, and one that was more legitimate, was older teens that were officiating games in which their younger siblings were playing. This was an accident waiting to happen but we were aware of it early enough to make scheduling changes. For the most part, we dodged that bullet fairly well. Later, we were able to budget for and make this a paid position for these youth referees. It not only gave them a chance to make a little money and to give back, but it also gave them a chance to see the game from the other side of the fence. Soon we established a high school league that would give these teens an opportunity to referee a game at eight o'clock and play in a game at nine.

You Play Like You Practice

If the challenge of scheduling games for all these teams wasn't enough, we also had to schedule days, locations, and times of practices. There wasn't much school gym space or timeslots left but we did what we could. Practice times were only about ninety-minute blocks of time, which made planning essential. The practice had to be instructional, interesting, and disciplined, yet fun. We also needed to consider the players' various levels of skills and interests.

One of the teams I coached was particularly challenging when it came to explaining and executing strategies, especially on defense. I was trying to get the team to execute a defense that would collapse around the middle, bottling up opponents who liked to drive up the middle. We really had trouble making it work until I used the analogy of the Venus fly trap. From then on, anytime I needed the defense to collapse on the opposition in the middle, I would just yell, "Fly trap," and it was executed to perfection. The girls thought it was great fun.

The high school team was greatly influenced by watching college and professional sports. I have noticed that the offense on these teams often centers around one individual who tries to dribble through all five players on the defense while everyone else stands around watching him. In my attempt to eliminate dribbling and increase the amount of passing in our games, I created a special drill. When we scrimmaged, I would instruct the team that they had to keep the ball from touching the floor for five minutes at a time. That's right, no dribbling, only passing was allowed. If the ball touched the floor, the other team would take possession. On occasion I also added the challenge that no one could shoot until everyone on the offense had touched the ball at least once. What started out to be my own reaction to the frustration of excessive dribbling turned out to be a valuable drill.

Coaches as Role Models . . . or Not

Sport was invented to satisfy the human urge for competition. Competition, whether on the football field or behind a chess board, can be an enjoyable experience between friends or it can turn into a multiheaded monster. If left unattended and with enough kindling, you could turn a child's basketball league into the lions against the

Christians in the Roman Coliseum. From year to year it could turn a wastebasket fire into a two-alarm blaze.

At first we had games and schedules, just enough information so that teams knew where to go and who they were playing, where, and at what time. Each bench kept score in their own book, and every once in while someone from the bleachers would yell, "Hey, what's the score?" and they would get an update. We also decided, as coaches, that we would inform the crowd at the end of every period. Things were pretty civil and games went on relatively well until the first piece of additional fuel was added.

1. The Electric Scoreboard

Bad idea! Good thought, but fuel for the fire. Every second of every game, you can see who is ahead and who is behind and by how much. You can watch the digital representation of time ticking agonizingly away and with it, the eventual demise of the team with fewer points.

Once we all got used to it, it became a passive indicator of where we were, but it had no real influence on the game at first.

2. Published Scores and League Standings

Okay, I'm sorry; this one turns out to be my fault. With every good intention, my previous efforts to secure software to make scheduling all these league games easier and more accurate also had the additional feature of collecting actual scores and turning them into league standings and personal statistics, such as who scored more points than who. Now on the surface, this again is not bad in itself. Somehow, these meaningless statistics get translated into the first-place team having a better record than the other teams. But it also gets twisted into my first-place team is better than your second-place team. My first-place team is smarter than your second-place team. My son is better than your son, my daughter is prettier than your daughter, and my dog is bigger than your dog. Can you feel the flames starting to get higher?

3. *League Playoffs*

Fueled by expansion in the Major Leagues, playoffs, wild card games, sudden death, and March Madness, we continued to fan the flames and introduce yet another fuel source to the competitive process. This fuel is called playoffs. It was apparently not enough that we had standings at the end of the regular season as to who had the most wins and fewest losses, and who eventually had the fewest wins and the most losses, but we now had to expand this into a new level of "I'm better than you."

Coaches and directors went back into our smoke-filled rooms to come up with illogical parings of who was going to play whom in the first round, the second round, the quarterfinals, the semifinals, and the final. The consummate tournament playoff has to be March Madness and the NCAA basketball tournament. Here, out of hundreds of eligible Division I college basketball programs, sixty-four teams are picked to play each other. In a frenzy of games across this great land of ours, we narrow the field quickly to thirty-two and then to the Sweet Sixteen and then the Elite Eight, and then the Final Four. The Final Four is then reduced to the championship game amid national fanfare between the two teams remaining. The winner is then declared the national champion. Now that's a playoff. I knew reverse binary was good for something!

Before I leave March Madness, I also need to address the concept of team pairings. You see, those sixty-four original teams are divided into four regional groups of sixteen throughout the country. East, West, South, well, you get the idea. Initially, each of those regional teams has to be scheduled to play one of the other teams in that sixteen-team division. Each game after that is dictated by who won, who lost, and who is left standing. This first game, however, needs a system to determine who plays whom.

I know, let's do it this way.

Let's take the top team, the number-one team in each division, and have them play the worst team in that division, the sixteenth-ranked team, if you will. We can then have the number-two seed play the number-fifteen seed, and the number-three seed play the number-fourteen seed, and so on. That will ensure that we have such a mismatch in the first round that the average teams that just made it into the tournament don't have a snowball's chance in hell of making it past the first game (although there have been miraculous exceptions).

With that brief explanation as background, let's go back to the smoke-filled room to design a playoff schedule for our league using the same type of absurd criteria. If you are playing or coaching in this league, it means you have at least an average interest in sports. As a sports fan you have watched and understand the implications of the playoffs, the championship, the World Series, and so on. The very nature of this new postseason schedule takes on a more urgent, competitive, and carnival-type atmosphere. Walking into the gym for the first game, you can actually feel the room temperature has gone up ten to fifteen degrees.

There was a plus side to this escalation of competition: it has the potential to build character and create unforgettable moments for players and coaches alike, as long as it is recognized and used with the bigger picture in mind. I am not advocating that we stop keeping score or stop having playoffs, even in elementary school leagues. I am saying that we need adults, parents, and coaches to see the bigger picture and to guide younger, less experienced, and more vulnerable children through the experience. The fact is, even as children, we are all going to experience a time when there is more competition, when the stakes are higher. From making the final cut for the middle school cheerleader squad, to joining the debate team, to applying to college, to being offered a job when your spouse and two children are counting on you. You need to understand that no matter how high the stakes are, it's not always going to go your way.

4. *Tournament Fever*

With each passing game, the field of teams grows smaller. Eight teams become four and then two. As each team was eliminated, the players would come to the next game and sit in the bleachers, supporting one team or another. Attendance for these games grew almost 300 percent from the regular season games. As the competition became more intense and the field grew smaller, the fans became more polarized and unforgiving. We weren't into a game for more than a few minutes where there wasn't something wrong with everything. The coaches were unfair, the referees were blind, the scorekeepers weren't paying attention, and even Mom's dinner that night wasn't up to snuff.

One particular playoff game stood out above all to summarize the ugly side of playoff competition. The game obviously was going to be too close to call in the final thirty seconds, and any mistake, bad call, or great individual play could be the difference. The game did end on a close call and a one-point victory with a small scuffle between two players. The scuffle turned larger and moved itself over to the bench area just below the bleachers packed with parents. These postgame festivities eventually blossomed into the two head coaches pushing and shoving and at one point punching each other in front of shocked parents and siblings sitting in the stands.

The ironic thing about this ugly display of poor sportsmanship was that the sons of each of the coaches broke up the fight by physically pulling their fathers apart. As league director, I had always thought that if it ever did come down to fighting, it would be the fathers pulling the sons apart and trying to set the example.

Everyone likes to win; everyone wants to be the champion. No one likes to lose. The reality of competition, however, is that for every winner, there has to be a loser. The team or individual that comes up a run short, a stroke behind, or a second from the lead is always going to be declared the loser. Sometimes there is a reasonable explanation, and sometimes there isn't. One of the greatest coaches of all time, Vince Lombardi of the Green Bay Packers, said, "Winning isn't everything, it's the only thing." Now, that may be a great pregame motivator, but what happens when you are sitting in the locker room, dirty and bleeding and on the short end of a heartbreaking loss? What happens after all that? Losing is the reality, even though you've done everything right. What do you tell your team?

As a coach or a player, you have to come to grips with only one thing: Did I do my best? Did I give it everything I had in the heat of competition? Giving your best in sports, or just in life, has little to do with how talented you are, how skilled, how fast, or how muscular. We all have our own talents and levels of ability. It is how you used what God gave you in that moment in time that becomes the true victory, the true glory, and the memory that will live on long after everyone has forgotten the score. A twelve-year-old may not understand this, but if you plant the seed, if you paint the bigger picture, even though tear-filled eyes can't see it, the words will be valuable when they are ready. It is those moments that are the gold nugget in the prospector's pan of sand and water. These precious moments are few and far between, and if we can let our children and young adults know ahead of time when these moments present themselves, they won't miss them as they go by.

The High School League; New Challenges

There was another interesting challenge about the time a young athlete goes from eighth grade in middle school to freshman year of high school. Many young athletes who had participated regularly in team sports enter high school with some desire to play on a high school team. My son Matt was no exception.

Football is usually the first sport on the school calendar. Matt considered football briefly. Most guys who decline to go out for the football team do so because they think they are not big enough to play. Others bow out because of the physical contact and the rough nature of the sport. Not Matt; he indicated thumbs down on football when he found out he had to be at the school at eight o'clock and go till noon. The team was allowed to go home and have lunch and then had to be back on the field by two o'clock for a session that lasted till five. The look on Matt's face could only be interpreted one way. "Are these people insane? I have better things to do than to spend all day practicing something I already know how to do." Somehow, Matt was referring to a practice schedule that I remember when I was in high school. A practice session that said, "Football is a team sport and more importantly, an extracurricular activity which should be part of a well-rounded curriculum." Somehow, through the constant hype of local press and demands of scholarships to college, the stakes started to rise on the success of high school athletics. In any case, Matt had a life beyond football, and he was going to pursue other options.

It wasn't the end of the world, however, because a month or two later, it was time for basketball tryouts. Matt was coming off of a better-than-average few years playing basketball in our town junior and senior league. This would be the perfect opportunity to extend his involvement in sports.

There were three tryout sessions for the high school freshman basketball team. Each was held in the gym, and unlike previous teams, the parents were not allowed to observe. To me, the dedicated sports fan, and my sons' most avid cheerleader, that made about as much sense as not letting the father in the delivery room! The coaches wouldn't even socialize or talk after practice. It was obviously a secret society, which we the parents were not privy to or intelligent enough to understand.

The three tryouts came and went, and then the coaches disappeared behind closed doors for a few days to decide the fate of those who bared their physical souls to be on the team. Who would be selected, and who, like the World's Biggest Losers, would be sent home? Several days went by, and then a rumor leaked that the selections would be made on this particular day. I remember Matt in his room, with the door closed, pretending to do homework. Around eight o'clock that night, the phone in his room rang (no cell phones yet). I could hear Matt mumbling and mostly listening through his closed door. I wasn't breathing, partially so I could hear better and partially out of anticipation. Finally, I could hear the phone click, and I dashed into the kitchen, where I could assume an innocent, unconcerned posture. Matt walked in and announced, with little change in his expression, that he had made the team!

The good news was that Matt was a member of his freshman high school basketball team. The bad news was that so were eighteen other boys. I don't know how much you know about basketball, but there are five players on the floor at a time. If you have three, four, or five other players as substitutes, you have an effective roster. What we had here was the equivalent of three basketball teams in one. Needless to say, for most of the season, a good portion of the team was doing the same thing that I was doing at the game: watching!

Apparently, the secret society of closed-door coaches decided the tryout sessions were really not part of an elaborate selection process. Since the coaches obviously weren't interested in developing individual players as much as they were making a name for themselves, they quickly decided who the best seven players were, and those were the only ones who saw playing time. As you might expect, other players began to quit the team in search of more involvement, more fun. Great job, coaches!

Selecting a player to the team and condemning him to a year on the bench was far crueler than cutting him loose and allowing him to chase other interests.

Our Town High School League

About this same time, a few of us involved in our local town's basketball league were entertaining the idea of extending our league, which already included a biddy team and two girls' teams, besides the original junior and senior boys' teams. We wanted to include a league for high school players. Little did we know at the time that the fiasco going on with high school sports was providing plenty of fertile ground for our idea.

Although we had many interested players, it wasn't really enough to start an entire league. In order to jump-start the league, the board decided to open it up to neighboring towns, as long as each participant had a birth certificate and parental approval. Oh yes, and if I failed to mention it before, I was elected league director.

Now looking back, I have to say that this was probably an exercise in spreading yourself too thin. I was already coaching a senior league team with Jim, and John had just entered the junior league as an eight-year-old. If I wasn't cheerleading in the bleachers, I was coaching, directing, or administering.

After some brief local advertising and recruiting, we were able to conduct a tryout session for interested candidates. Because we needed as many players as we could get, the tryouts were not to eliminate candidates but more to assess skills so that teams would have some degree of parity. The last thing we wanted were teams that beat other teams by fifty points.

We were able to conduct reasonable sessions with the help of interested parents and former coaches. When the dust cleared, we had six teams. Not only was there a mix of teens from our town and neighboring towns, the league was also coed. We many girls interested in playing but not enough for a separate league. To add some competitive flair to the league, we decided to use team names from the NCAA Big East conference. Our teams included the

UConn Huskies, Syracuse Orange, Boston College Eagles, and St. John's Redmen.

The initial response to the league was very positive. The logistics of a high school league were a special challenge. Because we decided to open the registration to neighboring towns, we weren't as familiar with some of the talent coming to the initial tryouts. The league progressed with a minimum of issues for the first year.

Since I was one of the founding fathers of this league, I not only inherited a coaching job, I was also the logical choice of league director. I was surprised at how much bigger and more physical these kids were, especially those in their junior and senior year. According to their birth certificates, some of them were closer to nineteen than eighteen by the time the season started. Many of our league meetings centered on logistical issues rather than the games themselves. Because many of the players were old enough to have a license, they often drove themselves. Many of them came to registration without parents and permission slips, and we had to turn them away or have them come back with a parent.

Word quickly spread, and soon other teens, especially from out of town, wanted to be on the teams that their friends were on. It was clear that by opening up the league to out-of-town players, we had inadvertently created a monster. We decided on a cutoff date, and during the next two years of the program, we instituted enrollment, tryout, and placement rules to ensure that these newcomers weren't stacking a particular team behind our backs.

For the most part, the games were very competitive, and our team, the Demon Deacons, fared very well throughout the season. Balancing the team and developing the players was no easy task. I developed two different offensive units, Gold and Black, after our team colors. The Gold offense and defense was taller and more stable in terms of play-making and execution. The Black team was smaller but faster and more aggressive. I found that alternating these teams at strategic times during the game not only ensured that everyone got their required playing minutes, but that we were also giving the other team fits trying to keep up with us.

Trouble in Paradise

The games were competitively physical, and I was constantly worried about how the girls were going to hold up under these conditions. We were constantly reminding all the coaches that they not only had to ensure that the girls received just as much playing time as the guys, but that there was also a reasonable amount of decorum to these games. We did have occasional fights and some heated exchanges between players and referees.

By midseason, the temperature of these games became so heated that I called a special coaches meeting. We knew that these games were getting more and more physical and it was critical that coaches and referees kept a close eye on the action and also listened for "trash talk." This taunting would go back and forth and then, almost without any other warning, would quickly escalate into a fight.

The next night, we had a regularly scheduled game with the Eagles. Prior to the game, I talked to the opposing coach, and we agreed to remind the players about taunting and fighting. It was exactly fifty-three seconds into the game that the first punch was thrown. So much for team meetings.

Fans in the stands were another issue to be managed. During junior and senior division games, the vast majority of spectators were parents and siblings. They watched the games, read the paper, or otherwise conversed about parental stuff while younger brothers and sisters sat in the bleachers, coloring or getting a jump on their homework. Not so with the high school games. Apparently there is an unwritten rule for some parents: "Once your sons and daughters get to high school, you don't have to support their interests or achievements anymore." We had at least two players on our team who, in three years in the league, never had a parent attend one of our high school games. This void was filled with friends and friends of friends who would drive to these games unsupervised and sit in the stands to yell and sometimes heckle their friends and the opposing team. This new development provided some security and game control issues that we never experienced before.

Enter the Police

By the second year of the league, we had things running fairly smoothly with schedules, practices, and game results. The automated software that I tracked down a few years earlier continued to allow us to revise schedules and provide weekly updates on scores and standings. We found out through the grapevine that the local police department had a makeshift team that played in a local recreational league. Our board thought it might be a great bonding experience for our local teens to play a few exhibition games with the police team. It would not only give our teams a few extra games, it would also allow the police to become more familiar with these local teens, many of them new drivers. It sounded like a "win-win" for everyone.

The first few games went very well, and I believe at one point we were even mentioned in the local newspaper. Yes, things were going well, until one of our teams actually beat the police! After that, it seemed like the proverbial manure had hit the fan. Those games became more competitive, more verbal and heated, heavily seasoned with taunting from the large crowd of team followers.

Just when I thought things couldn't get any more challenging for our league, I started getting calls from parents. Yes, these were the same parents who had not attended the games, now calling me and complaining about these additional games. I was quickly reunited with a truism that I had known for years: No good deed, or even a good intention, goes unpunished!

We tied for the league championship that year, and in our second year we had a good team also. The same dynamics that ended my tenure as a baseball coach started to dissolve my secondary calling as a basketball coach and league director. Matt graduated high school and left the program. He had come a long way from that first team picture as a junior: the big toothy smile flashing the peace sign as an eight-year-old and finishing ten years later as an eighteen-year-old young man, ready to take on college and the world. Jim transitioned into high school basketball, baseball, and track and thus elevated himself from the inner workings and politics of the local leagues. So it was for our youngest son John, who found a home and a legacy with high school soccer and track. John would go on to become All State in both sports and set records for the school and the league.

The next year I had no family ties in the league, and although I could hear myself saying that the best coaches I ever saw were the ones that had no children playing, I was tired and ready to end it.

Along with the fact that my sons were no longer in the league was the realization that I was rapidly losing my passion and excitement for sports. I was spending more time breaking up fights, cleaning up beer bottles in the parking lot, and trying to satisfy unreasonable parents who never bothered to attend a game than I was enjoying the essence of the games. The most disappointing aspect about this changing of the guard was the remarkable lack of interested or dedicated parents to which we could pass the torch. I am not sure how the general public thought that registrations and tryouts were conducted, schedules compiled, uniforms ordered, games supervised, statistics recorded, and even banquets arranged, but apparently they didn't think volunteer parents had anything to do with it. Yes, there are always exceptions, and there were parents willing to help in some capacity. It just seemed at the time that that small army was getting smaller.

I had the pleasure of working with two great sports figures in our local community: Charlie V for baseball, and Tom C for basketball. Charlie loved baseball and was an influence at many levels. His efforts helped to really grow Babe Ruth baseball in our town. Tom was similar to me in many ways in that he had enough own sons to start his own basketball league. He was coaching multiple teams in multiple divisions, and he was also on the board, ordering uniforms, and fighting with schools for space. Tom was the only other person who was familiar with our scheduling software, and as I continued to become less of a force on the court and on the board, he even taught his sons how to produce an entire season schedule on the computer.

As far as we had brought the league and with the innovations that we tried and in many cases succeeded with, I was reacquainted with a concept I was familiar with even back in the days of pickup games at Thomas Hooker School: Sometimes things run better and kids have more fun if parents just stay out of the way. I look back on the high school league and wonder if we would have been better off just opening up the gym, throwing in a few basketballs, and letting the local teens loose for two hours of pickup games. It worked for us when I was sixteen.

My original motivation for starting the high school league was to provide an opportunity for local teens interested in sports to prolong their day in the sun just a little longer. The fact is that I wanted to extend my sons' days in the sun a little longer. I wanted to move beyond the muddy pit of high school athletic politics and keep the game alive for as long as possible. That last year turned out to be my coaching swan song in baseball and basketball.

After that year, I transitioned from coach to fan. I had come full circle. I had started as a five-year-old fan. I gradually entered into a long and glorious age of participating in sports, being part of the drama, thrill, and agony of the games. I rode that wave as long as I could, well into my forties, and then I became a coach. Now I had come full circle, back to being just a fan.

The next few years we spent watching our boys participate in everything from pickup beer softball games to state tournaments. I took sick days and killed off the same relative so many times it wasn't funny just to see a game. It didn't matter whose game it was or what was at stake. It was a last gasp at being a part of the sports that I loved, and the sports I grew up with.

Beth and I would sit at these games watching our sons, now grown men, long after other parents of twenty-five-year-old sons had gone off to the golf course, moved to Florida, or were at home converting their son's bedroom into a den or a "man cave." Yes, we would be at these games, sometimes watching from our car or a distant bench behind a tree, trying not to embarrass them with other friends.

With all the great memories, disappointments, and eventual disillusionments, I wouldn't have traded any of it for anything. I walked into Dunkin' Donuts the other day for my morning coffee. As I was walking out the door, I looked up to see a well-dressed man probably in his thirties with a smile of recognition on his face. He looked at me and said, "Hey, Coach!"

CHAPTER 5

Twenty Reasons Why It's Hard to Be a Sports Fan

Sports always seemed to be one of the pure, untouched natural resources in my life. There was a time when the baseball World Series was played between New York subway stops. We had many teams in many sports, but there was a consistency and a loyalty in all of it. That loyalty and passion for the game gradually started to erode away. Part of that erosion was just the onset of adulthood and shedding some of the naïve mind-sets of a twelve-year-old. Legitimate erosion was caused by overcommercializing professional sports until it had lost all its flair for sports and became a business. Free agency started the ball rolling. It decimated established teams. The BCS followed, along with an exponential expansion of professional leagues. Look, they play pro hockey in Canada, Boston, New York, and Chicago, but Florida?

There are many reasons why it's hard to be a dedicated sports fan these days. Here are my top twenty, in no specific order.

Jim Chernesky

Reason 1. March Madness:
You can't have it both ways.

One of the truly maddening things about sports is the preoccupation with rankings, especially in college, the BCS, and certainly NCAA basketball. Last year's NCAA tournament was a classic example.

Throughout last season, we carefully watched the top twenty-five basketball teams jockey in and out of contention for the number-one spot in the nation. ESPN darlings such as Duke, Ohio State, and North Carolina were tracked, reported on, and talked about for the entire season. Imagine the utter disappointment when mediocre UConn, who barely limped into the Big East and NCAA tournament and then "ran the table" on the last eleven games to win it all. This unexpected national champion flew in the face of many media sports analysts, and even the president of the United States had his tournament bracket busted. I had to rip mine up early in the tournament also. This is not an advertisement for UConn basketball. Syracuse came from basically the same obscure back-of-the-pack position to win it all in 2002. The point is, if you want your top four media favorites to play for the national championship, then make the tournament just the Final Four and be done with it. The beauty of sports is that if you have a tournament with sixty-four teams, there is always a chance the team that is ranked last in the tournament could win it all.

Yes, I know we as a nation are obsessed with this massive elimination process that drags on forever. We also watch bachelorettes whittle down twenty-five equally handsome contenders in a superficial display of true love and lasting devotion.

Back to basketball. I think it is clear after last year's tournament that these week-to-week rankings mean next to nothing during the course of the season and only serve to come up with a system to create pairings for a national tournament that has too many entries.

Rankings and bracketing just give us something to talk about while waiting for March.

Reason 2. NFL game analysis paralysis.

When I was a boy, my father and I would come home from church in the fall and head upstairs to the attic. We would walk up the attic stairs to make our necessary pregame adjustment of our television antenna. After opening the upstairs bedroom window, we would proceed to loosen the bracket on our television antenna, mounted conveniently outside the bedroom window. I would hand my father tools, and he would carefully undo the brackets and rotate the antenna slowly to the worn pencil mark on the bracket. This mark indicated maximum reception of the New Haven stations, which were the only ones broadcasting the New York Giants home game in a blacked-out New York market.

Once the game began, we would watch a black-and-white rendition of the game without color or HD video. If you were to watch that game with me now, you would see some unique sports oddities.

First, back then, the quarterbacks called their own plays, only conferring with the head coach on rare occasions. The head coach's job was to stroll up and down the sidelines in an overcoat and Dick Tracy hat, smoking a cigar and yelling at anyone in earshot.

Second, there were no on-field microphones and little color commentary. You couldn't hear the plays in the huddle or the very detailed explanation of the last penalty (or the jersey number of the violator, because after all, we have to attach blame to everything these days). Instead of this audio barrage, viewers would watch the referee signals that indicated the infraction. Not only did you have to understand the game and the rules, you also had to know what these signals meant.

Finally, and most obviously, there was no instant replay! Whatever the outcome of the last play on the field was, that was the final decision. Whatever the call, it stood carved in stone for all eternity. If you went into the kitchen for another beer, you missed it. There was no agonizing delay while scores of striped-shirted officials hid under black-hooded cameras, looking at repeat footage at a speed so slow that the grass grew quicker. However, there was also less need for instant replay because the officials were much more skilled at calling penalties than they are today. People with at least a partial knowledge of the sport they are watching can only look on in disbelief at the calls that are missed. To make matters worse, the only way to compensate for such a lapse is to make an equally horrible call against the other team within five minutes of the first call.

Now don't misunderstand me; I think new technology has the potential to add many benefits to watching sports, but in most of these examples, it's a clear example of the tail wagging the dog. Overhead cameras and telescopic lenses bring you right onto the field and into the huddle, but the quality of the game, strategy, and even the officiating sometimes leaves something to be desired.

Reason 3. How many pitchers does it take to finish a baseball game?

Having grown up at a time when baseball was the primary sport on television, I quickly became a true lover of the game, even at the early age of five. I remember sitting in our living room watching the Brooklyn Dodgers and the New York Yankees in the midfifties.

Time and again I would watch pitchers like Whitey Ford spend nine innings (yes, I said nine innings) completely baffling the opposition with a nasty combination of carefully selected pitches that were choreographed by veteran catcher Yogi Berra. Incidentally, Whitey was five foot, nine inches and couldn't have weighed more than 170 pounds on a good day. He didn't use steroids, and his diet consisted of beer and hot dogs with Mickey Mantle after the game. Whitey typically did not stop pitching until the game was over. No one was counting his pitches or giving him medical attention between innings (other than putting on his warm-up jacket and changing the chewing tobacco in his mouth).

Today, starting pitchers are only cleared to pitch the game after they reach the mandated four days rest between starts. Pitchers who aren't knocked out of the box by the fourth inning usually only cruise along until the sixth inning, when they reach one of baseball's "hard stops": the dreaded seventy-five-, eighty-, or eighty-five-pitch rule limits how many pitches you can throw.

Don't despair, however, because baseball pitching rotations now have what is strategically referred to as a setup man. These pitchers enter the game during the black hole created in the sixth, seventh, and eighth inning, long past the physical limits of most starting pitchers these days. Notice that I did not refer to the ninth inning, because that is the job of the closer.

The closer is another in the cast of characters it takes to pitch a Major League game these days. The closer's job is to pitch the ninth inning of the game; occasionally, if he feels really ambitious, he might be brought into the game to pitch the last out of the eighth inning as well as the ninth.

Now for those of you who don't understand true baseball strategies, there are other supporting cast members that you need if you are going to pitch your way through to the end of a baseball game. At any time while a setup man or a closer is pitching, there may be extenuating circumstances that would require one pitcher to leave the game and be replaced by yet another pitcher.

For example, apparently it is either a federal offense or a mortal sin for a right-handed pitcher to face a left-handed batter after the sixth inning of a baseball game. If the setup man is right handed and a left-handed batter is due up, the manager must instantly jump out of the dugout, run to the pitcher's mound, and summon a left-handed reliever. "Why?" you ask. Because statistics and physics basically argue that it is more difficult for a left-handed batter to hit a left-handed pitcher, or so it is written.

However, this strategy creates a new dilemma. Because in the natural order of life, the next batter coming up may be right handed. The right-handed batter, left-handed pitcher combination is equally frowned upon, and since we don't want to get on the bad side of either the federal government or the Vatican, you know what we need to do. That's right, we need to stop the game again, come out, and remove the left-handed pitcher (who has only thrown three pitches to the left-handed batter) for a right-handed pitcher.

For those of you fans that have actually witnessed this phenomenon, you know that it is not unusual to see three different pitchers in one inning. If you wanted to extrapolate this nonsense throughout an entire game, then do the math. Your formula is nine innings times three pitchers an inning equals twenty-seven pitchers in a game (and don't even consider what would happen if the game went into extra innings). Cousin John or Aunt Mary would have to be called in to pitch. We have taken a relatively simple coaching consideration of starting pitcher and relief pitcher and turned it into a cast of many.

True baseball fans know I have probably exaggerated here, but not really. Consider this true story:

Circa 1975, I watched a game on television between the New York Mets and the Philadelphia Phillies. It was a pitchers' matchup between two legends, Steve Carlton for the Phillies and Tom Seaver for the Mets. For eight solid innings, these two greats went head to head like heavyweight boxers, going blow for blow. Both pitchers were closing in on twenty strikeouts going into the ninth inning. As the last inning unfolded, it was amazing that no one was counting how many pitches these two pitchers had thrown, no manager came out of the dugout to check on blisters or sore arms. The catchers on both sides had stopped giving signs to the pitchers, because all they were throwing was unbelievable fastballs anyway. No mixing of pitches, no deception, just pure, take-your-best-shot, come-and-get-it power.

Even more amazing, during this last inning I looked out at the respective bullpen. There were no pitchers warming up, no one taking off their jacket to prepare to warm up. The only real activity was a card game or two that was left unattended while everyone pulled their chairs up close to the fence to witness this incredible exhibition.

The game ended 2–1. I don't remember who won the game, but that's not important. It was one of the most incredible competitive displays of strength, desire, determination, and love for the game that I have ever witnessed in professional sports. Neither pitcher was concerned with relief or even a contract extension.

I am certainly not the first one to admit that there is managerial strategy attached to professional sports. I know that as a coach, I have been involved in my share. What has happened, however, in the course of a game is that the complexity of strategy and change, sometimes just for the sake of change, surpasses and outweighs the opportunity for the physical playing of the game to unfold. At some point, you have to make your best move and let them play the game!

The other downside of all this is that the responsibility of the game's outcome begins to shift from the players to the manager or coaches. More and more postgame press conferences are televised, so that the manager and the hero or goat are put on the postgame pedestal or chopping block for a public verbal autopsy on why things did or didn't happen and why they lost the game. In every game, there is a 50 percent chance that your team is going to lose. If both teams won the game, no one would watch.

Reason 4. When did it become a crime to get dirty? Artificial turf.

Okay, this is where I may start to sound (in the words of my wife) like "an unreasonable crabby old man," but there is something sacrilegious about playing any game on artificial turf. Let's go all the way back to the early sixties when the Houston Astros, or then the Colt .45s, began play in the Astrodome, the first stadium to install artificial turf. The first problem that this high price tag undertaking created involved Nellie Fox, a former All-Star second baseman who was the first-base coach for Houston. Nellie always appeared on the field with a huge chaw of tobacco puffing out his left cheek; he looked like a squirrel on a good nut day. The problem: there was no place for Nellie to spit his tobacco. Groundskeepers actually had to place a brass spittoon out in the first-base coaching box to contain the foul brown liquid.

On a more practical note, the artificial turf made the ball move faster, especially on the ground, and additional injuries in both baseball and football occurred because of knee and ankle injuries. The simple reason for this is that when your foot is planted on natural grass, it provides some resistance against your leg or knee; the grass or sod usually gives and relieves the impact of running or getting hit in football. No such luck with artificial turf. The carpet doesn't give; your knee or ankle absorbs the impact, often with ugly results.

My biggest problem with artificial turf is more aesthetic. Football was meant to be played outside in the elements. Once upon a time (before domed stadiums) the NFL's Thanksgiving game shown on television was usually played between the Detroit Lions and the Green Bay Packers. Now, think about Michigan (or worse yet, Wisconsin) during the last week of November. It is a meteorological fact that the sun doesn't shine at all up there during November and December. What makes matters worse is that it is either raining or snowing or both. The field usually looked like a set for modern-day mud wrestling. By the third quarter, you not only couldn't see the white hash marks on the field, but the uniforms on both sides were completely indiscernible. You couldn't tell one team from the other. (Ahhhh, that was football.) You could tell the rookies or the second-stringers in a game like this, because outside of the punter, they were the only ones with clean uniforms. I ache to see just one more game like that.

I have to admit that there are advantages to artificial turf, especially since they have made vast improvements to make it safer and more realistic-looking than the old carpet in the Astrodome. I will concede artificial turf but I am sticking to my guns on shiny pants. Football pants were supposed to be made out of white cotton. I was watching the New Orleans Saints one Sunday, and they all, to a man, had shiny (and I mean shiny) gold football pants. What I saw on television made my blood run cold. It was a 320-pound bald trapeze artist with a number on his back.

Reason 5. Somebody always has to win (no ties).

Historically, football, soccer, and hockey games at every level were hard-fought battles and sometimes ended in a tie at the end of regulation. Now, I hope you're sitting for this next part. In some cases, the game actually ended as a tie. No sudden death, no overtime, no shootout, just a tie. You could look at a team's record and see something like 6-2-1. Six wins, two losses, and a tie. Somehow we used to be okay with that. In this age of reality television, we have this need to pare everything down to the lowest common denominator, the final contestant left standing after we have tearfully eliminated every other contender on the horizon. This mind-set expands itself into what we witness in college bowl games. On New Year's Day, there used to be four well-established bowl games to enjoy on TV. The champions of each conference would pair off for one final exhibition to cap off the season. Each of the four bowl games was an event unto itself and had no bearing on the other three. The Rose Bowl, for example, was between the winner of the Big Ten conference (with the likes of Michigan, Ohio State, or Michigan State), and the winner of the PAC 8: Southern Cal, UCLA, Stanford, and so on. There were four winners, one from each bowl game. Mankind then looked down upon what it created and said, "No, that will never do, we can't leave the season with four winners, we need an ultimate number one, a national champion and ultimate standalone top-of-the-heap team."

Enter the Bowl Championship Series (BCS). Now we have a computer-driven system that makes automated decisions about who plays who and eventually decides which final two teams play each other, outside the framework of the bowl games, for the coveted national championship. This system takes into consideration wins and losses, strength of schedules, weather reports, and how the bluefish are running in Long Island Sound. Meanwhile, we have two or three other legitimate contenders to the title, with similar and often undefeated records, who stand on the outside looking in at all this, wondering why they are not playing in this game.

Reason 6. When did coaches stop running the team?

As I continued along the road of life from childhood to adult, I saw the sports world continue to grow beyond its moralistic boundaries. Like a snowball rolling downhill, growing larger and more encompassing with each revolution, so has it been with sports. Baseball, football, and basketball leagues started to expand. Major League Baseball almost doubled in size, the American Football League, the American Basketball Association, not to mention hockey and the increasing popularity of soccer. With this type of growth came vastly increased media coverage and intense competition from up-and-coming college and high school athletic protégés vying for these additional career opportunities. The positive side of this was that we were able to witness some of the greatest athletes, teams, and games of the modern era.

The disadvantage of all this was that, in some respects, the beast had grown to such a size that it started to destroy itself from the inside out. Multimillion-dollar contracts for virtually untested rookies created a larger-than-life image that established them as a franchise player. Instead of being part of the team and part of the organization, they *became* the team and the organization. They rose above the rules and expectations for the other members. We have seen examples where these prima donnas have actually influenced or superseded a coach's authority and even threatened their jobs. There is a natural order to sports. The coach or manager runs the team and makes out the lineups, not the general managers. The quarterback calls the plays, not some shirt-sleeved assistant coach in the press box. Sportswriters pick the All-Star teams and the Hall of Famers, not some seventeen-year-old girl who thinks the Yankees shortstop is cute.

Reason 7. Is anybody out there healthy enough to play a whole week?

A few years ago, I was invited to join a baseball fantasy league. A fantasy league is a computer-generated league that mixes the Major League players and provides you with a roster of players and pitchers, which you follow as part of the regular baseball season. As the games are played, you capture actual statistics of the players on each team: home runs, batting average, stolen bases, wins, strikeouts, pitching saves, and so on. Those statistics are compared to the other teams and players that make up the league, and standings are created just like the real thing. For sports and baseball fans, it is an intriguing way of simulating the management and day-to-day running of your own baseball team. Participants get to make trades of players and decide how best to use the talent on their team.

The thing that makes this activity interesting is the day-to-day actual performance of all the players. Hopefully, if the league is run correctly from the original draft of players, most of the teams have a fairly equal distribution of talent. In the real world, however, there is usually a difference from season to season between the potential of the talent you have on your team and its actual performance. A player who had a stellar season the previous year sometimes fizzles out in the current season. Similarly, players who did nothing in the prior year can do no wrong this year. These leagues are always interesting because that element of the game is always anyone's guess.

There was one variable in this season-long activity that was frustrating enough to make you throw up your hands and turn to basket weaving. I would faithfully pull up my roster before every game and begin to set my lineup and select my pitcher for the next game. I would consider who my team was playing and where and make the best strategic decisions based on sound baseball knowledge and gut feeling. As I scanned the daily roster, I was disappointed to discover that at least a few times a week, one of my players, usually a key player, had a red "DL" next to his name. The dreaded "DL" stands for disabled list, which means that player has sustained some type of ailment, usually a pulled this or a sprained that, which keeps him on the bench and out of your game plan. There were days when there were enough red "DLs" on my roster list to look like some sort of summer Christmas decoration.

Today's twenty- or thirty-something weekend athletes and fantasy managers take all this in stride. However, there are those of us who remember Cal Ripken. Cal Ripken played in 2,632 consecutive Major League Baseball games for the Baltimore Orioles without missing a game. No, Johnny, that is not a misprint. I said 2,632 consecutive games without missing a game. For those of you (including me) who have trouble getting a handle on how long that is, I will put it into perspective for you. Cal Ripken started his streak in 1982, a month before my oldest son was born, and ended the streak in 1997, three months after that same son graduated from high school. No, I am not making this up!

So the question, in my mind at least, is, "What is the difference?" Cal was made of the same basic body parts as the players of today. He had no bionic arms or legs, and he certainly didn't have access to the same performance enhancers that today's warriors have. You can't even blame it on the motivation of additional compensation. The year he started the streak, his annual salary was $33,000. If anyone out there has a plausible explanation for this, I would love to hear it.

Reason 8. Five-on-one basketball.

If there is a hell, and I'm pretty sure there is, it would be finding me tied to an armchair and being forced to watch an endless stream of professional basketball. We pick two of the most popular, publicized teams and then find the two most popular players on both teams and let them wage a personal war against each other. This war is waged by dribbling the full length of the court, making wild acrobatic shots while the other eight guys on the floor run around, waving their arms and displaying their sweaty tattoos.

Now there are plenty of basketball fans who are going to hate me for that comment . . . but come on, guys, if you want to teach your firstborn the game of basketball, you must have a better teaching tool than watching pro basketball. If I had a dollar for every senseless foul, full-court pass that went ten rows back in the bleachers, or selfish showboat display, I could retire tomorrow.

Reason 9. Red Zone football on Sunday.

Imagine playing chess with a board filled with all queens or rooks, all pieces having the same high-level power with no distinction in rank or ability to influence power and strategy. Imagine an ice cream sundae that was all whipped crème, no ice cream, no fruit, bananas, chocolate syrup, or nuts. So it is with Red Zone football on Sunday afternoon, compliments of your favorite sports channel and cable network. For those of you that are not familiar with the football term "Red Zone," allow me a minute to explain. The Red Zone refers to the area of the football field inside the ten-yard line. When a team is inside the opposition's ten-yard line, the probability is that within the next few plays there will be some sort of scoring opportunity.

Now, holding onto that concept, imagine a typical Sunday during football season; the National Football League has thirty-two teams. If all but two play on Sunday (don't forget Monday Night Football), these means there are sixteen games. Don't you love math? Now because of geographic proximity and optimum marketing opportunities to make millions, all the games are not televised at once. Half of the games are shown in the 1:00 p.m. slot, and the other half are in the 4:00 p.m. slot.

Are you still with me? Good! That means that there are a few games going on at the same time. You start to watch the game of your choice and presto, you are transported to an entirely different game because one of the teams has entered the Red Zone and is about to score. In short order, you witness some sort of scoring opportunity and then, in less time than it takes to run a commercial, you are whisked away to yet another game, not the original game you were watching, but this new team has an opportunity to score since they are now in . . . yes, you guessed it, the Red Zone. Unless they are totally inept, they come away with a score. Once again, we are taken to yet another game that presents a scoring opportunity. Hence, all the other aspects of the game from good defense to special teams play and yes, even a quick peek at the NFL's most treasured resources, the cheerleaders, is lost in the barrage of scoring plays.

With this wonderful perspective on the game, you can probably witness a few hundred points being scored all over this great land of ours in the time it takes to eat a bucket of wings and drink a beer. You have just experienced a Sunday with all whipped cream. I suppose there are plenty of sports fans, yes football fans, that prefer, and in fact love, Red Zone football. To me, sitting through a session of Red Zone football is like sitting in a room with a flashing strobe looking at black light posters. Oh, and one more thing: anyone who really knows and appreciates football in its complete and unabridged entirety knows that some of the most exciting scoring plays strike like lightning at the most unexpected times; they have little or nothing to do with the Red Zone. If you're sitting with a son, daughter, sister, or brother, watching football, please decide on one game and watch it. Ultimately, they will enjoy it more and learn more.

Reason 10. Where are all the sports idols? (Where have you gone, Joe DiMaggio?)

Drug dealers, rapists, wife beaters, gamblers, and the list goes on of prominent sports figures that make the headlines. Children growing up absolutely need an idol, an older adult to look up to and emulate. In a perfect world, it should be a parent or a priest or a close family friend. It's okay to have another prominent public figure to fill that slot. In today's society, it can be very difficult to find that person. The reason is we have taken every notable figure, sports star, movie celebrity, or political hopeful and chipped away at their best qualities and well-meaning positive exterior until we get down to a skeleton in their closet, such as a poor (and sometimes immoral) decision they made. It is very difficult to find someone to look up to these days that has not aired more than their share of dirty laundry.

Now, I'm not saying that former stars, politicians, and movie stars were saints. Mickey Mantle was known for his extracurricular activity, Paul Horning (the Golden Boy) was a known gambler, and even JFK had his own list of indiscretions. The point is, when they were in the limelight, very few people knew about these issues. Children who looked up to these people certainly didn't. Information can either be used for positive or negative outcomes. I go back to the old adage, "If you can't say something good about a person, don't say anything." The next thing they will be telling us is that Santa Claus carries illegal substances in his toy bag.

Reason 11. Here today, gone tomorrow (free agency and arbitration).

Sports always seemed to be a rock, something steadfast that I could count on, but somewhere around the mid-1960s the rocks started to move, and my world began to shake. I think the first sign of this change was one day when I turned on the television to watch a New York Yankees game and Mickey Mantle was at first base instead of center field. Things seemed to go downhill fast after that. Tom Seaver (Mr. Met) eventually pitched for Cincinnati; Johnny Damon was traded from the Boston Red Sox to the New York Yankees, which is like oil and water, and then to Florida. Joe Montana was traded from the San Francisco 49ers to the Kansas City Chiefs. Brett Favre was sent from the Green Bay Packers to the Minnesota Vikings. The straw that really broke the camel's back was Peyton Manning going to the Denver Broncos from the Colts. I don't care what the reason . . . the world has gone mad!

Reason 12. You need a second mortgage to take your family to a live professional sporting event.

I will never forget the first baseball game I attended. When I was eight years old, my father took me to Yankee Stadium to see the Yankees play the Washington Senators. By the way, the Senators became the Minnesota Twins two years later, and a new expansion team became the Washington Senators. Then one of them, yes, I think it was the new Washington Senators, became the Texas Rangers. God, someone give me a Louisville Slugger so I can bash myself in the head. Anyway, back to my point. I will never forget, in the days of black-and-white TV, walking through the portal at the stadium and seeing the field in color for the first time. If there was ever a baseball cathedral, it was the old Yankee Stadium. I can never really verbalize the experience adequately to anyone, but Billy Crystal, the actor, does a great job describing it in the movie City Slickers. Billy says, "I'm seven years old, and my dad takes me to Yankee Stadium. My first game. We're going in this long dark tunnel under the stands, and I'm holding his hand. We come up out of the tunnel into the light. It was huge . . . how green the grass was . . . brown the dirt, and that great green copper roof, remember? We had a black-and-white TV, so this was the first game I ever saw in color. Sat through the whole game next to my dad, taught me how to keep score, Mickey hit one out." That day we paid $3.50 a piece for box seats on the third-base line. If you wanted to sit in the bleachers, it cost you 75 cents. The only reason you wouldn't want to sit there is that most of those seats were 450 feet from home plate and there was no big screen in center field. Did you know that from that distance the ball is actually traveling for about two seconds before you hear the crack of the bat?

I finally fulfilled my lifelong dream to take my boys to a game. It cost us $80 apiece for tickets and $75 to park the car. Did you know that if you give a vendor a twenty-dollar bill for two hot dogs and a beer, you don't get change? I love sports as much as the next guy, but I have to tell you that the game I saw for $3.50 was better.

Reason 13. Your favorite college basketball team will only include freshmen and sophomores.

Good news! Your favorite college basketball team, after months of aggressive recruiting, has landed one of the nation's top high school basketball prospects. Bad news! After a stellar freshman season, and possibly hanging around for his sophomore year, depending on how long it takes him to make up his mind, that stellar basketball candidate will be whisked away by the professional draft. The potential draftee will sit with his college coach and give him perfectly plausible reasons on how he has to leave school for the multimillion-dollar contract. If it was up to him he would stay, but his family needs the money.

I wonder how many actually stay in professional basketball and how many, after a round robin of trades, become insurance salesmen? In the meantime, college basketball fans everywhere are left with this revolving door of flash-in-the-pan talent. You have to scratch your head when you realize that these universities go to such an extent to secure this talent that the schools are often fined and coaches suspended. You would think the universities would try to hang on to these treasures a little longer.

Reason 14. The Roger Maris syndrome: Once you do well, nothing else you do will ever be as good!

Roger Maris was an average outfielder for the Kansas City Athletics in the late 1950s and into the 1960 season. He was traded to and became the right fielder of the awe-inspiring New York Yankees. During the 1961 season, Roger Maris paired up with his centerfield counterpart Mickey Mantle (where have I heard that name before?) to stage one of the greatest home-run races professional baseball had ever seen. Maris and Mantle, or the "M&M boys," as the media called them, went neck and neck, homer for homer, chasing Babe Ruth's immortal record of sixty home runs in a season.

I was an avid Yankee fan and an eleven-year-old Little Leaguer at the time, and this was certainly a bittersweet baseball season for me. In one respect, these teammates provided enough offense for the Yankees to beat the rest of the American League into submission and then pound the Cincinnati Reds in five games in the 1961 World Series. The downside of this battle was brought on by sports fans and the media who seemed to resent that this out-of-town new Yankee was challenging the great Mickey Mantle. As the season wore on, and the two edged closer to the record, Maris began to receive threatening letters from fans. He was hounded by the media and often put into difficult situations with himself and his teammates. Mantle started to slip behind Maris and eventually fell out of the race due to extensive injuries; the pressure, the threats, and the conflict only grew worse for Maris. How dare this young upstart outdistance the great Mick and threaten the Babe's home-run record!

Maris did eventually tie and then break Ruth's record of sixty home runs, although baseball found a way around that by saying that because Ruth had done it in 154 games and Maris did it in the newly expanded league schedule of 162 games, his record would bear an asterisk. If you are really interested in this story, see the movie *61*, which accurately depicts the emotional and physical side of this memorable sports conflict. After the 1961 season, Roger Maris's career steadily went downhill; he was later traded to the St. Louis Cardinals and eventually vanished off the radar. Despite the fact that he still had decent seasons, nothing he could ever do would be good enough after 1961.

This was, for me, one of the first signs that there was a dirty, vindictive back room to sports that went unnoticed by eleven-year-old Little Leaguers, but for older youths and adults, it started to peek out ominously from behind the joyous innocence of the sports that I loved.

Reason 15. Minneapolis to LA, Brooklyn to LA, Oakland to LA, and back to Oakland

Do you know why the Los Angeles Lakers are called the Lakers? You're going to love this! The Los Angeles Lakers used to be the Minneapolis Lakers; where is Minneapolis? That's right, up by the Great Lakes. It's a pretty creative name for a team from Minnesota or Michigan or Ohio, for that matter. It doesn't quite do the job in Los Angeles, but let's not stop there. The Oakland Raiders' owner decided to pack up his team and move them from Oakland to Los Angeles. When everyone realized that the team name Raiders meant just as much or as little in Oakland as it did in Los Angeles, he moved the team back to Oakland!

Last, but certainly not least, one of the most devastating team moves for sports fans was the once iconic Brooklyn Dodgers moving from Brooklyn out to sunny Los Angeles one fateful day in 1957. To this day, I always suspected that the Brooklyn Bridge was built just for that day when so many die-hard Dodger fans considered jumping off a bridge.

The Baltimore Colts snuck out of Baltimore in the middle of the night for Indianapolis. Why do they make it so hard to be a fan?

Reason 16. Gotcha! We always need someone to blame.

There is no sport where this following phenomenon is more prevalent than professional football. I am referring to the mind-numbing practice by network television and the press of singling out the victim of the last on-field mistake and making them the topic of conversation over the next five minutes of the game. The quarterback who just threw an interception, the kicker who just missed a game-winning field goal with four seconds left, the punt returner who fumbled away his team's last chance to win the game are all on the media hot seat. First, and this is relatively new to televised football games, the referees will not only announce an infraction but also report the uniform number of the violator in question. It used to be enough just to announce, "Holding on the defense." Next, the camera will zoom in on this individual we have just put a media dunce cap on and follow him as he sheepishly makes his way back to the huddle or the bench. If that weren't enough, three plays later we are still providing video flashbacks of this person, even if he is now sitting on the bench by himself with head in hands. These mistakes are just as much a part of the game as kicking the winning field goal, scoring a touchdown, or recovering a fumble. This is why end zone celebrations are such a pathetic and plastic part of the game. You never know when the fickle finger of fate will turn on you in the middle of a critical game. The game has a way of leveling the playing field.

It just occurred to me that we can't blame sports for this performance autopsy that the media feels is fair game. This attitude goes all the way to Washington. Thanks to bipartisan politics and self-serving public figures, we have a system now that is more interested in establishing blame and making sure that it is on someone else than actually working to solve the problem.

Reason 17. Defacing the sacred baseball cap.

The baseball cap has long been a sign of allegiance to your favorite team and a tribute to your favorite players. You wanted the cap to look like and be worn just as the Major Leaguers did. About the only thing that was different was that we creased the cap just above the team logo on the front of the cap. For some reason, it looked cool, even though the Major Leaguers, for the most part, didn't crease their caps.

There is now a store in most malls that sell caps exclusively, or a variation of it. Here you can buy just about every kind of sports team cap. "Why do you need a whole store just for caps?" you ask. Well, let's take the typical Yankee cap for instance. The traditional Yankee cap, as long as I can remember, was navy blue with the white "NY" interlaced on the front of the cap. Now, you can get that same cap in about eight different colors. I have seen it in green, yellow, and, God help me, pink. I have seen the Yankee cap tie-dyed and camouflaged. If that wasn't enough, most young fans today wear their cap backward. Catchers used to be the only players who wore their caps backward, in order to accommodate their mask. Now, most kids wear their caps backward. To me it's like flying the flag upside down.

While we are on the subject of baseball uniforms, let's look at uniform pants and socks. Baseball uniform pants were designed with elastic to end about midway down your shin. There it met your baseball socks coming up from your shoes. They usually met about halfway between ankle and knee. Under the socks were white socks that were displayed like a white horseshoe rising up from the laces on your baseball cleats. Some players wore them higher or lower, depending on style and preference. Bob Allison, All-Star slugger of the Washington Senators and Minnesota Twins, wore his socks all the way up to his knees. Now this, to a knowledgeable baseballer, was more than just a fashion statement. When a batter is standing at the plate, and the umpire is calling balls or strikes, he knows that the strike zone on a batter runs from his chest down to his knees. Anything above the letters or below the knees is a ball. Allison's high socks created an optical illusion, which actually shrunk his strike zone and made umpires call pitches right at the knees balls instead of strikes. Pretty smart, huh?

The next time you turn on a Major League game, look at that same pants-socks relationship today. The uniform pants go all the way down and back on top of the shoelaces. There is no sign of a sock to be found. It looks sloppy, and worse, it has got to be tough to run with the pants flopping at your feet. Has anyone seen my Louisville Slugger?

Reason 18. Letting the fans pick the All Stars.

Once upon a time, the Major League Baseball schedule was divided in half. It started the first week in April, and the leagues began their 150 game schedule, playing day in and day out. The halfway point between the beginning of April and the end of September is roughly the Fourth of July, give or take a few days. As we got closer to the season's midpoint, cigar-smoking, derby-wearing sportswriters sat at their Underwood typewriters and pored through the latest statistics and schedules. These men who ate and drank sports would methodically go through all this information and, with two parts head and one part heart, select the Major League Baseball All-Star teams that would play the showcase game in July.

Today, we have ballots that the average guy or girl on the street can use to pick the All-Star game participants for that year. The only prerequisite is that you have a computer, can access the Internet, and can click a computer mouse. You don't even need to know anything about baseball.

Reason 19. Losing becomes a personal, in-your-face statement.

I'm sorry, but here is another one I can't sit still over. One recent Sunday morning, I was reading the sports page, which included headlines, stories, and pictures from the previous day's NFL playoff games. The headline at the top of the page read "Brady Silences Tebowmania with Six TD Passes." Now for those of you living on a distant planet (or if you are reading this book fifty years from now), let me clarify. The headline refers to the New England Patriots beating the Denver Broncos 45–10 in the AFC playoff game. Now, the last time I checked, there were roughly about forty-four players on each NFL team when you count offense, defense, and special teams. My question is, "How did an eighty-eight-player football game whittle itself down to a two-man gunfight?" I'm not a Tim Tebow fan. I can't say I am a Tom Brady fan either. I do know that this was about the Patriots beating the Broncos, not Brady beating Tebow. It's obvious that the press and the fans have taken this whole game, and even the concept of honorably winning or losing a football game, and managed to degrade it down to an inner city street fight. I think I'll see what's on the Hallmark station.

Reason 20. Participating in sports and games is fun until adults and parents take over.

Throughout the pages of *Once a Fan*, I have recounted childhood memories about playing after-school pickup games with my friends. We defined and accepted our own rules, secured locations and equipment ahead of time, and played the games, for the most part, without any major altercations. We even had ways to ensure that if there were too many (or too few) players that day, we were still able to pull off some fairly enjoyable competition, win or lose.

As I grew older, I began to see a pattern. The amount of fun that I had was inversely proportional, and the amount of confusion and conflict was directly proportional, to the amount of involvement that parents or adults provided. The consummate example of this, and the best way I can describe it, was the seemingly harmless event called the Cub Scout Pinewood Derby.

The derby was an opportunity for eight-, nine-, and ten-year-old Cub Scouts to build a miniature racing car from a predesigned kit. The car was made out of a block of pinewood, cut out to represent a car body. It included four plastic wheels and two thin metal axels. It also came with rough assembly directions and some rules on what you could do and what you couldn't do during the building process. The ultimate goal was to build, paint, and test your own racecar and then bring it to the monthly pack meeting, where fifty or sixty scouts would race their cars to determine the ultimate winner.

There were tools involved at a relatively young age, so parental supervision was required. Because it was common knowledge that there could be sixty contestants but only one winner, this proved to be a recipe for disaster. Parental supervision quickly turned into fathers building cars while Cub Scouts watched passively or left the room to find an activity that was more fun. Cars were cut with lathes and band saws instead of handsaws. Secret lubricants were used on wheels and axels, and some were painted with a nonfriction lacquer paint that was shinier and more aerodynamic than our family car.

The ultimate insult occurred during the pack meeting, when most of the fathers ended up with a lot more input into the race itself and ultimately argued over the winner and the prizes. This event, similar to the Miss America Pageant, had one winner and fifty-nine losers. With a little thought, we could have had multiple awards in different categories, including Most Futuristic, Most Original, Best Red Car, and so on. Alas, we could only have one winner, like Miss America.

There are probably more than twenty reasons why it is hard to be a sports fan, and certainly some out there that I haven't thought of. I am not a pessimistic grumbler by nature (despite what my wife says), but I think if we were going to do some sports house cleaning, I submit these as my recommended twenty places to start.

CHAPTER 6

The Sensational Seven: My Most Memorable Sporting Events

We have all had life experiences that stirred up our emotions and moved us to the very soul of our being, experiences that have renewed our faith, heightened our desire, and strengthened our will. They have brought chills to our spine and tears to our eyes. For each of us, they are different. My only wish is that everyone has an experience like that once in a while. It can be, using the famous quote from the movie *The Maltese Falcon,* "The stuff that dreams are made of."

Since this book is all about my lifelong experiences in sports, how they affected me positively or negatively, and how I used that as a positive influence on others during my life's journey, I couldn't leave this chapter out. "The Sensational Seven" takes a look back on the seven most memorable sporting events I have had the pleasure of witnessing. I would be remiss if I also didn't include my thoughts on what I learned and took away from them. They are not meant to be 100 percent accurate but to provide enough detail to illustrate the monumental tribute that these games were to the world of sports.

Here, then, are my Sensational Seven:

1. 1955 World Series:
Brooklyn Dodgers versus New York Yankees

The Subway Series, as it was christened, was always a fan favorite, and the 1955 Series promised more competition than the previous meetings had. The Dodgers lost seven World Series in the past; the last five had come at the hands of the Yankees.

Don Newcombe, a twenty-game winner during the regular season, was called in for the Dodgers to start Game 1. Sometimes, even when you lead with your best, you come out on the short end. Despite a strong effort, the Dodgers lost the first game, 6–5. Even as a young Dodger fan, I felt the psychology of being down early in the Series. But there was always tomorrow. Well, tomorrow came and went, and Tommy Byrne, a thirty-five-year-old left-hander, held the Dodgers to only five hits as the Yankees took the second game, 4–2. The beautiful thing about sports, however, is that as frustrating as it is to have your best go down to defeat, there are always unexpected surprises from the young and inexperienced. Just as the Brooklyn faithful were on the verge of giving up hope, an unlikely hero named Johnny Podres took the mound. Podres had struggled to a 9-10 record for Brooklyn and was set to go up against the Yanks' seventeen-game winner, Bob Turley. A better script could not have been written for the occasion as the young man (on his twenty-third birthday) lit up Ebbets Field with a clutch 8–3 win that put his teammates back in the Series, only down 2 games to 1.

The Dodgers' momentum continued in Game 4 as Roy Campanella, Gil Hodges, and Duke Snider all added homers for an 8–5 victory that tied the Series up at two games apiece. Brooklyn added to the streak in Game 5 when rookie pitcher Roger Craig worked six-plus innings for a 5–3 decision that put the Dodgers ahead for the first time. Could this be the beginning of the end for the great Yankees dynasty? The Yankees showed why they were true and consistent champions, however, coming back for a 5–1 win in Game 6 that was complemented by an incredible four-hit effort by Whitey Ford.

Dodgers' manager Walter Alston decided to start his Game 3 hero, Johnny Podres, in the decisive Game 7, while Yankees manager Casey Stengel selected Game 2 winner Tommy Byrne. There is no rhyme or reason to making these last game decisions. The season spans five months and about 160 games. As a manager, you make decisions like this with part of your head and a good deal of heart and gut. For Alston, it was a conflict between finishing with the percentages of using your best and most experienced, or going with your gut and betting on the kid, Johnny Podres.

Despite surrendering eight hits and two walks, Podres managed to hold the Yankees scoreless and entered the ninth with a two-run lead. He held on in the ninth, forcing an easy fly ball to left and two routine infield ground balls to end the game. It was over! The Dodgers had finally beaten the Yankees for their first world championship title. The "Bums from Brooklyn" would win another National League pennant the following year, but their days were numbered, and they would play only two more seasons in Brooklyn before moving to Los Angeles.

Postgame Thoughts

I have to admit I don't remember much about this game, since I was only four. I do remember how my father was such a passionate, die-hard Brooklyn Dodger fan. I remember how the formidable New York Yankees always seemed to walk away from the Fall Classic with the ultimate prize. This year would be different. Game 7 of the 1955 World Series was too close to call, even with a Dodger two-run lead in the seventh inning. Amazing too was the performance of Johnny Podres, pitching in the World Series against the mighty Yanks. I didn't really grasp that accomplishment until I was twenty-three, trying to imagine myself standing on the pitcher's mound in the seventh game, or any game, against the New York Yankees of the fifties.

This was also a bittersweet time because a few precious years later, the beloved Brooklyn Dodgers, the "Lords of Flatbush," moved to Los Angeles to start a migration of teams out West. It would be the last championship the Brooklyn Dodgers would ever play in. It was double heartbreak knowing that at about the same time, Roy Campanella, All-Star catcher for the Dodgers, suffered a severe auto accident, paralyzing him for life. It was one of those times in life that leaves you scratching your head trying to answer the question, Why?

2. 1958 NFL Championship: Giants versus Colts

Both the New York Giants and the Baltimore Colts finished the 1958 season with a 9-3 record. For the Giants, it was their fifth consecutive winning season, a stretch that included an NFL championship in 1956. In contrast, 1958 was only the second winning season in Colts' history since the team's founding in 1953.

The 1958 NFL championship game got off to a rough start for both teams. Most of the first half was peppered with fumbles and good defense big plays that turned the game into a back-and-forth slugfest. Even stars such as New York Giant halfback Frank Gifford were guilty of fumbles and mistakes that caused these two great teams to pass opportunity back and forth to each other in the first half. There were times where mistakes were turned into advantages in some of the most unlikely ways.

At one point, late in the first half, the Colts drove eighty-six yards in fifteen plays, including a sixteen-yard scramble by Unitas on 3rd and 7. Unitas was never known for his ability to run, but this was a game in which everyone reached back for that something extra. The Colts eventually found more opportunity and scored right before halftime for a 14–3 lead.

The second half continued the drama in great fashion. The Giants then went ninety-five yards in just four plays, scoring on Mel Triplett's one-yard touchdown run to cut the lead to four points, 14–10. The Giants then went ahead early in the fourth quarter on a fifteen-yard touchdown pass to Frank Gifford. On the next two Colt drives, they moved the ball into scoring position but did not score. After trading desperate attempts to get some type of offense going, the Colts took over at their own fourteen-yard line, and Unitas engineered one of the most famous drives in football history—a two-minute drill before anyone called it that. This set up a twenty-yard tying field goal by the Colts with seven seconds left to send the game into sudden-death overtime, the first in the history of the National Football League. At the beginning of the overtime period the referee explained to both teams, "The first team to score, field goal, safety, or touchdown will win the game, and the game will be over."

As darkness and the cold of a late December evening settled in over Yankee Stadium, these two champions prepared to slug it out to the finish. It was the Colts who finally managed to put a scoring drive together. The memorable part of this sudden death overtime was the subtle but consistent performance of the Colts. There was no one individual who carried the team. It was Don Maynard, Ray Berry, Johnny Unitas, and Alan Ameche and others who pulled together to take the ball down to the Giants one-yard line. Ameche scored on a third-down touchdown run to win the game, 23–17. This drive is considered one of the best in NFL history.

Postgame Thoughts

It still brings tears to my eyes, this game. It was only in black and white on television, but in the overtime period, I could feel the cold night of Yankee Stadium and see the vapor coming from the mouths of exhausted players. There was no replay, there were no sideline interviews, but these two teams were so evenly matched that they just refused to lose.

I remember the happiness yet confusion of the game-tying field goal. Although games could end in a tie, a championship game certainly couldn't. To see two team captains go back out to the field for the toss of a coin to continue playing an overtime period was unheard of. I have to admit, I was a Giants fan and Frank Gifford was one of my football heroes. As much as I was pulling for the Giants to win in overtime, I could tell by the gritty determination of Johnny Unitas and his surgeon-like execution of the last drive that the Giants were never going to see the ball again. When Alan Ameche took the ball in from the one for the game-ending score, it just plunged a dagger into my heart.

On the positive side, this game truly did put professional football on the map. It created an undeniable curiosity and popularity to football that didn't previously exist. Four years later, the American Football League debuted, paving the way for the first Super Bowl. I have to wonder if the AFL and the Super Bowl would even exist if it weren't for "the Game."

3. 1960 World Series, Game 7: Pittsburgh Pirates versus New York Yankees

The 1960 World Series was a classic David-and-Goliath matchup. The Pittsburgh Pirates had managed to hang on through six grueling games to force a seventh and deciding game with the mighty New York Yankees. For the seventh game, Bob Turley, the winning pitcher in Game 2, was picked as the starting pitcher for the Yankees against Vern Law, who had won Games 1 and 4 for the Pirates.

The Pirates came out early with good hitting and established a seemingly comfortable 4–0 lead after four innings. In true style, the Yankees roared back in the fourth and fifth inning with an impressive hitting attack and two home runs, taking the lead, 5–4.

The game seesawed through the later innings, both teams getting clutch plays and hits from some of the most unlikely heroes. The Yankees increased their lead, only to see it evaporate to a 7-6 edge. Just when it looked like the Yankees were back in control, Hal Smith of the Pirates launched a three-run home run to give the Pirates a 9-7 lead.

Bob Friend, an eighteen-game winner for the Pirates and their starter in Games 2 and 6, came on in the ninth to try to protect the lead. The Yankees' Bobby Richardson and pinch-hitter Dale Long both greeted him with singles, and Pirates manager Danny Murtaugh was forced to replace the veteran pitcher in favor of Harvey Haddix. Although he got Roger Maris to foul out, Haddix gave up a key single to Mickey Mantle that scored Richardson and moved Long to third. Yogi Berra followed, hitting a short grounder to first, with Rocky Nelson easily getting the second out. In what, at the moment, stood as a monumental play, Mantle, seeing he had no chance to beat the play at second, scurried back to first and avoided Nelson's tag (which would have been the third out) as Gil McDougald (pinch-running for Long) raced home to tie the score, 9-9. If the Pirates had turned the double play, the run would not have counted. With the run in, the top of the ninth continued but ended when the next batter hit into a force play.

Ralph Terry returned to the mound in the bottom of the ninth. The first batter to face him was Bill Mazeroski. With a count of one ball and no strikes, Mazeroski cracked a historic home run over the left field wall, ending the game and crowning the Pirates as World Series champions. As the Pirates erupted, the Yankees stood across the field in stunned disbelief. The underdogs had been outscored, outhit, and outplayed, but they had managed to pull out a victory anyway.

Bobby Richardson of the Yankees was named MVP of the Series, the only time that someone from the losing team has been given that honor.

Postgame Thoughts

I was in fourth grade in October 1960. Before the extreme commercialism that engulfed professional sports in later years, all World Series games were played in the afternoon. Because the games were in October, any self-respecting school-age sports fan was in school during the games. With the almost-hometown Yankees in the Series with the Pirates, it was not uncommon to find a few of us die-hard sports fans hiding a transistor radio under our desk.

Even if you don't follow baseball, looking at the box score of this last game tells the story of a back-and-forth slugfest. Just when you thought the Pirates were done, they came back with a rally. Just when you thought the Yankees were finished, they stormed back to retake the lead. The last two innings of this game were probably the most amazing and dramatic two innings I have ever witnessed.

The saving grace in all this was my mother. My father was working at the time, so she took it upon herself to record the audio play-by-play of the game, in its entirety. Thanks, Mom! I did manage to run home from school for the ninth inning. Again, as a Yankee fan at this point, I was pulling for extra innings and a Yankee rally to end it.

I ran into the house to see Ralph Terry had just come into the game as a relief pitcher for the Yankees, and he was facing the bottom of the Pirate batting order: Bill Mazeroski, the second baseman. I was relieved for only one pitch. The second pitch Mazeroski hit on the nose with that undeniable wooden bat sound. To this day, I can hear:

There's a long drive to left field, Look out now. . . . That ball is going, going, gone, and the World Series is over.

—Mel Allen, Yankee
announcer

The Pirates were decisively outscored in the Series but managed to hang on. The Yankees would win a game 15–2, and the Pirates would win the next 2–1. The Yankees would come back and win the next 10–0, and the Pirates would win 3–2. Years later, Mickey Mantle was quoted as saying that losing the 1960 Series was the biggest disappointment of his career, the only loss, amateur or professional, that he cried actual tears over. Legendary Yankee manager Casey Stengel was fired at the end of that season and replaced with Ralph Houk. For me, losing Casey was the end of another chapter in baseball. For Bill Mazeroski, by contrast, it was the highlight.

4. 1975 World Series, Game 6: Boston Red Sox versus Cincinnati Reds

This game would go down as one of the greatest games, not only in World Series and postseason history, but baseball history as well. Thanks to three days of rain in Boston, Red Sox manager Darrell Johnson had the luxury of using his best starters, Luis Tiant and Bill Lee, for Games 6 and 7 to try to hold off the mighty Cincinnati Reds.

The Red Sox took the lead in the first inning on Fred Lynn's three-run homer off Reds starter Gary Nolan. Meanwhile, Luis Tiant breezed through the first four innings, holding the Reds scoreless.

The Reds finally scored in the fifth. With two on, Ken Griffey tripled to deep center, scoring two runs. Johnny Bench singled Griffey home to tie the game at 3-3.

In the seventh inning, George Foster put the Reds ahead with a two-run double, and in the top of the eighth, César Gerónimo hit a home run to give the Reds a 6-3 lead.

In the bottom of the eighth, Bernie Carbo, an unlikely hero, tied the game with a three-run home run just to the left of dead-center field.

The Sox looked poised to win the game in the bottom of the ninth, but the Reds were able to hold off the Red Sox rally and end the inning with no runs scoring. The two teams battled on through the tenth, eleventh, and twelfth innings while trading heart-pounding attempts to take the lead and end it, but the score remained tied.

In a fitting end to such an exciting game, Carlton Fisk, the Red Sox catcher, came up to bat facing Pat Darcy, the eighth pitcher that Reds manager Sparky Anderson used. Fisk hit Darcy's second pitch and lifted a high drive down the left-field line. The ball struck the foul pole just above the Green Monster in left field. In what has now become an epic baseball highlight, the television camera caught Fisk wildly waving his arms to his right after hitting the ball and watching its path while drifting down the first-base line, coaxing the ball to stay fair. The ball indeed stayed fair, and the Red Sox had tied the Series.

Postgame Thoughts

There were two elements to this game that not only made it one of the classic games of all time, but one of the most memorable for me. The first was that from the very onset of the game, everyone on both sides gave 110 percent for the entire game. Fred Lynn's home run in the first inning did not cause any head-hanging on the part of the Reds. They chipped away at Boston's three-run lead, and by the eighth inning, they had actually gone ahead. Boston, also undaunted, came back to tie it and send the game into extra innings.

The second incredible observation I had made about this game was that the game reached a point where as a fan and spectator, it didn't matter who won the game anymore. The competitive spirit and mutual respect for both sides that surfaced in this game were unequaled in other games that I had seen to that point. At one point in extra innings, Pete Rose, Cincinnati's All-Star third baseman, allegedly turned to manager Sparky Anderson and said, "I don't even care who wins this game anymore, this is the greatest game I have ever played in."

Shortly after that, Carlton Fisk hit his memorable game-ending home run. If you ever get a chance to see that game on ESPN, don't miss it.

5. 1980 Olympic Hockey Game: United States versus Soviet Union

The Soviet Union entered the 1980 Olympic Games as heavy favorites in hockey. Their speed, experience, and team play were unmatched in this competition. The eventual matchup with the young upstarts from the United States would truly be a mismatch.

First Period

As in several previous games, the US team fell behind early. A pressure offense by the Soviets managed a shot past goaltender Jim Craig to give the Soviets a 1-0 lead, and after Buzz Schneider scored for the United States to tie the game, the Soviets scored again. With his team down 2-1, Craig played tougher, stopping many Soviet shots before the US team had another shot on Soviet goaltender Vladislav Tretiak.

In the waning seconds of the first period, Dave Christian fired a slap shot on Tretiak from a hundred feet away. The Soviet goalie saved the shot but misplayed the rebound, which bounced out some twenty feet in front of him. Mark Johnson sliced between the two defenders, found the loose puck, and fired it past a diving Tretiak to tie the score with one second left in the period. The first period ended with the game tied 2-2.

Second Period

The Soviets began the second period by replacing their goalie. The Soviet coach later identified this as the turning point of the game and called it "the biggest mistake of my career." The Soviet team allowed no goals in the second period and dominated play in the second period, but scored only once. After two periods, the Soviet Union led 3-2.

Third Period

In the final scoring opportunity of the third period, Mike Eruzione, who had just come onto the ice, fired a shot past the Soviet goalie, which was screened by the defense. This goal gave Team USA a 4-3 lead, its first of the game, with exactly ten minutes left.

The Soviets attacked furiously from then on. Moments after Eruzione's goal, they began to shoot wildly and in a panic as time was slipping away. With less than a minute left, a scramble for the puck ensued. As the US team moved the puck over the blue line with seven seconds remaining, the crowd began to count down the seconds left. Sportscaster Al Michaels, who was calling the game on ABC along with former Montreal Canadians goalie Ken Dryden, picked up on the countdown in his broadcast, and delivered his famous call:

"Eleven seconds, you've got ten seconds, the countdown going on right now! Five seconds left in the game. Do you believe in miracles? YES!"

Postgame Thoughts

I don't think I have ever watched a sporting event where the outcome was so predetermined in the eyes of everyone who witnessed it. I don't think I have ever seen a matchup that was so lopsided in terms of strength and experience. It was as though a local college football team was preparing to play the Super Bowl champions. Despite the fact that most US fans were prepared for a blowout, we couldn't take our eyes off the television screen for the whole game. It was as though you were witnessing a horrible traffic accident. You didn't want to look but you couldn't help looking.

Going into the last period, the US team was remarkable close, and when they tied it early in the third period, we seemed to sense that the ending wasn't going to be scripted as most people thought. I remember how fast the go-ahead goal went into the net, and my reaction actually knocked me off the sofa.

With ten minutes left at that point, I still had the feeling that this was too good to be true and that the Soviet team could rally and win. I never thought I could hold my breath for ten minutes. It wasn't until Michaels started his immortal ten-second countdown, "Do you believe in miracles?" that it started to sink in. It gave me goose bumps for a week.

6. 1986 National League Playoffs, Game 6: New York Mets versus Houston Astros

In one of the most famous games in baseball history, the New York Mets defeated the Houston Astros at the Astrodome, 7-6, in sixteen innings when Jesse Orosco struck out Kevin Bass for the final out with runners at first and second. This allowed New York to advance to its third World Series in their history.

Houston took a 3-0 lead in the first inning against Bob Ojeda with an RBI double by Phil Garner, plus RBI singles from Glenn Davis and Jose Cruz, giving Astros' starter Bob Knepper an early advantage. That lead held up for most of the game as Knepper was commanding, allowing no runs through the first eight innings. Meanwhile, Ojeda allowed nothing more through his next four frames, after which Rick Aguilera pitched three scoreless innings.

This set the stage for a Mets comeback in the top of the ninth. Lenny Dykstra, Mookie Wilson, Ray Knight, and Keith Hernandez all provided key hits in the ninth inning to rally the Mets back to a 3–3 tie.

Roger McDowell then came in to pitch for New York and allowed just one hit through five scoreless innings. Meanwhile, Houston pitchers Dave Smith and Larry Andersen held the Mets hitless until the top of the fourteenth, when Gary Carter singled, Darryl Strawberry walked, and Wally Backman singled off Aurelio López to plate Strawberry with the go-ahead run. With the bases loaded, Wilson struck out to end the threat.

The Mets were now three outs away from going to the World Series, but with one out in the bottom of the fourteenth, Billy Hatcher homered off the left-field foul pole against Orosco to tie the game, 4–4.

In the top of the sixteenth, the Mets strung together three key hits and scored three runs to pull ahead again, 7–4.

The Mets needed each of those three runs, as Houston rallied once again to make it 7–5. The Astros managed two more hits and another run to cut the Mets' lead to 7–6. Now with the tying run in scoring position, the winning run at the first base, and would-be Game 7 starter Mike Scott ready in the dugout, Mets relief pitcher Orosco struck out Bass to end the game and send the Mets to the World Series.

The time of the game was 4 hours and 42 minutes, and the sixteen innings was the most that had ever been played in a postseason contest at that time.

Postgame Thoughts

This for me was one of the last years I would really identify with an established team, one with a consistent lineup that you could identify and relate to. I was a Mets fan. This evenly matched playoff series had been an exciting one. This game was on a weekday, and I was frantically driving back from New Jersey in the eighth inning, believing I would not make it home in time to see the end. Bob Knepper, the Houston pitcher, was on fire this day, and the Mets couldn't score a run. Adding three runs in the ninth inning was not only highly improbable, it also pushed the game into extra innings. In fact, it was seven extra innings, almost a complete second game. Amazingly, the Mets finally scored in the fourteenth inning, only to have the Astros score in the bottom of the fourteenth. The Mets scored three runs in the top of the sixteenth and barely escaped after the Astros scored two in the bottom of the sixteenth.

I never believed in destiny before when it came to sports, but whenever the Mets were on the brink of defeat, they were able to come back. They would do it again later in the World Series against the Red Sox. Next to the seventh game of the 1960 World Series, this had to be one of the best baseball games I have ever seen.

7. 2008 Super Bowl:
New England Patriots versus New York Giants

After scoring a combined seventy-three points in their regular-season meeting, the teams scored a mere ten points by the end of the third quarter, with the Patriots leading 7–3. The Patriots' record-setting offense gave up five sacks and one lost fumble, while the Giants' offense managed only five first downs in the second and third quarters. In the fourth quarter, quarterback Eli Manning threw two touchdown passes, including the winning drive that culminated with a thirteen-yard touchdown pass with thirty-five seconds remaining.

After calling tails to win the coin toss, the Giants started the game with the longest drive in Super Bowl history, a seventy-seven-yard drive that consumed nine minutes and fifty-nine seconds. But New England halted the drive at their own fourteen-yard line, forcing the Giants to settle for a thirty-two-yard field goal that gave New York a 3–0 lead.

New England then responded with its own scoring drive; the Patriots returned the kickoff forty-three yards to the Patriots' forty-four-yard line. Quarterback Tom Brady engineered a precision drive, setting up a one-yard touchdown run on the first play of the second quarter for a 7–3 lead. On the Giants' first drive of the second quarter, they managed to move the ball down to the Patriots' nineteen-yard line before an interception stopped their threat.

Although both teams had explosive offensive weapons, it was always the defense that rose to the occasion, stopping scoring opportunities time after time. Although it seemed both teams could score at any time, the game went to halftime with the Patriots leading, 7–3.

During most of the second half, both teams traded opportunities and mistakes, mental and physical, and the contest raged on head to head.

On the Giants' first drive of the fourth quarter, Manning completed a forty-five-yard pass to rookie tight end Kevin Boss. Following three runs by Bradshaw and a seventeen-yard reception by Smith on third down, Manning finished the drive with a five-yard touchdown pass, giving New York a 10–7 lead with 11:05 left in the game.

After consecutive three-and-outs by the Patriots and Giants, New England got the ball at its own twenty-yard line with 7:54 to play. Brady engineered another precision drive of runs and passes, finally connecting with Moss, who was wide open in the end zone, giving New England a 14–10 lead with 2:42 left in the game.

The second half was filled with opportunities given and lost, mistakes, and big plays. Most incredible was the catch by Tyree. During New England's intense all-out defensive rush, Manning desperately managed to escape long enough to throw the ball toward the middle of the field, where Tyree and Rodney Harrison went up for it. Tyree made a leaping one-handed catch, outjumping

Harrison, and maintained possession by pinning the ball against his helmet as he fell to the ground.

A few plays later, Manning found Burress in the end zone, giving the Giants a 17–14 lead with just thirty-five seconds left.

New England had one last chance on their own twenty-six-yard line with twenty-nine seconds remaining and three timeouts, but the Giants' defense didn't allow a single yard, forcing an incompletion on first down. The Patriots never recovered from the last-minute Giants heroics.

Postgame Thoughts

I have watched an incredible amount of sports in fifty years. I have seen just about every Super Bowl since the Packers and the Chiefs squared off in the very first one in 1966. There have been tremendous games, but it's hard to pick one that was more incredible to watch than this one. Yes, I know it was only good if you were a Giants fan, but wait. The Patriots came into this game with a perfect, undefeated record. They were exceptional at just about every position on the field and had arguably the best quarterback in football. The Giants had been on a historic roll through the playoff and into the NFC championship game. Still, their quarterback, Eli Manning, had the reputation of being shaky and inconsistent. How would he stand up to the pressure of the Super Bowl?

The game was close, and even though the Giants pulled ahead in the fourth quarter, 10–7, there wasn't anyone, including me, who didn't think that the Patriots would pull it out in the end, no matter how much time was left. The Giants tried to mount a drive late in the fourth quarter and had it come dangerously close to stalling a few times. You knew it was only a matter of time before something happened that would seal it for the Patriots. It was like watching a lioness play with her food before she ate it.

It was only after Tyree's catch that you could feel that this was going to be a finish for the ages. If you haven't seen the catch, find it and watch it. It was a miracle that Eli Manning was able to avoid the savage rush and get the pass away at all. A few plays later, the Giants scored on another remarkable pass into the end zone and went ahead, 17–14, with about two minutes remaining.

I remember thinking, as the Giants kicked off to the Patriots for the last two minutes, *It's really a shame that the Giants are still going to lose this game after such an incredible, gutsy drive and the greatest catch of all time.*

New England began its last possession on its own twenty-six-yard line with twenty-nine seconds remaining and three timeouts. A closeup of Brady showed that he still had that confident sneer that said, "We got this." It was on the third-down play that you could finally see in Brady's eyes that they weren't going to pull this one out.

Even though the Giants won in an upset, this was one of the greatest games I have ever witnessed. I think if the Patriots had won it, I would have felt the same.

These seven games were more than just an incredibly exciting example of sports competition and grace under pressure. They were studies in character, of teamwork, and of fighting against all odds. In effect, they were real-world examples of some of the life lessons I will identify in the next chapter. These events will live on long after everyone forgets the score and the outcomes.

The wonderful golden years, my cherished days of playing and coaching the sports I loved, and certainly even these most memorable games would be just memories if nothing was learned and passed on. Whether you are a sports enthusiast or just an individual trying to make the most of your time here on earth, I hope you find something to take away in the life lessons that follow.

CHAPTER 7

Ten Lessons from Life

The old adage is true that sports provide many of life's lessons if you stop long enough to recognize them. I have looked at all the experiences, stories, friends, and people who influenced my life and have distilled them all down into ten undeniable life lessons. These ten truths have influenced me throughout my life, and I can honestly say that each one of them is just as applicable outside the sports world as in it. Here, then, are the ten lessons that I have learned:

1. It's not whether you win or lose.

I remember reading a quote from Joe Frazier, the boxer, which went something like this: "If I lose, I'll walk away and never feel bad. I did all I could do. There was nothing more to do." I know that is really small consolation for a high school kid who has just lost the league championship, but it will be a source of determination to go on when he or she has had a few of life's disappointments.

2. You're only as good as your last game.

One of the things I find particularly painful about watching professional football is the idiotic, egotistical, theatrical, and sometimes absolutely primitive displays of celebration after a touchdown, an interception, or some other individual play. Besides being demeaning to the sport, it is often the kiss of death. Many times, not long after one of these egotistical childish displays, the performer in question is involved in a mishap: a fumble, blown assignment, or other mindless display of poor judgment or stupidity that can turn a coach's hair gray. Going from hero to goat in thirty seconds is always a possibility in any competition, and it can make you look even more ridiculous.

In life, as in sports, you don't have time to rest on your past laurels. Even lives filled with accomplishments and fame can get stagnant. It's nice to look back on accomplishments but always with an eye on the future.

3. You'll never really appreciate winning until you know what it's like to lose.

I have been lucky enough to be the father of three amazing, wonderful sons who were great athletes in multiple sports. During their younger years, I coached baseball, basketball, and soccer to teach them the finer points of the games along with sportsmanship and values. One of the greatest lessons, however, I learned from them.

My youngest son John was particularly skilled in soccer. Although he did not have the advantage of highly structured training, he did manage to play varsity soccer in high school. Despite his lack of formal training, his speed, tenacity, and nose for the ball, combined with a complete disregard for his own physical safety, made him an incredibly exciting player to watch. All these attributes made him one of the most prolific scorers in the state; in fact, he led his high school team to the league championship.

His team played in the state tournament and did reasonably well until the quarterfinal game, where they lost a close but well-played game on a rainy night more suitable to ducks than soccer players.

Beth and I leaned on the fence surrounding the field in the driving rain, agonizing over the last two minutes, knowing John's team was not going to pull this game out. When the final horn sounded, ending not only the last game of the season but also the last game of John's high school soccer career, the players shook hands and made their way to the dry concession stand and waiting buses. As the lights went off one by one, only one lone figure was left standing in the middle of the field . . . head down and sobbing. John was crying, alone, by himself, not out of poor sportsmanship but out of the despair that comes when you know that you left everything you possibly could out there on that rain-soaked field that night and still felt responsible, that you could have done more.

We waited patiently in the rain by the fence for that one solitary player to come in out of the rain and couldn't help glancing over at the rest of the players on both teams. These players were eating and drinking and already planning the balance of their weekend, oblivious that they were missing one of their own.

It was then that I realized that the same drive, passion, and pride that made John so exciting to watch, the same drive that vaulted him to school records and state recognition, were the same traits that would not allow him to leave the field. I learned a lot about sports and a lot about life that night.

4. You can never go home again.

August 2012 will mark fifty years since we won the city's Little League tournament at Black Rock Field. Everyone once in a while, during those past fifty years, I find myself daydreaming, thinking back on that 1962 tournament, the last game, and wondering where all my teammates are now. On one such spring day, a good thirty years after that great season, I was driving back from a business meeting. As I drove along the interstate, I looked up to see the old water tower looming off to my right. I remembered looking out into the outfield from home plate and seeing that large water tower over the left center field fence about a quarter mile away. As I drove I thought, *Wouldn't it be great to see that field just one more time?* Almost as if another force was driving, I exited the interstate and drove toward that huge landmark. I drove across main roads and down side streets, trying to position the tower almost like an old homing device. When you are twelve and riding in the car to a game with friends, you don't really pay attention to street signs or landmarks. Although I didn't have a map, I knew I was close. I also knew the street, a dead end, started with a "W."

As I made another left-hand turn, I came upon a short street that looked like it could be it. I had a feeling in the pit of my stomach; I knew I had found it. With the tower ahead of me, and the river to my right, I knew I was just yards from the field that held so many great memories for me. As I pulled down to the end of the cul de sac, I looked up and my heart sank. I was staring at an old rusty fence. Beyond the fence was a large abandoned landfill with huge piles of garbage, old tires, and rusty bedsprings.

I sat there in the car with the engine off, just staring. What did I expect? Did I think I would see a Little League game in progress? Did I really expect to smell hot dogs and corn on the cob cooking in large metal pots? What I was realistically hoping for was a park with swings and children playing. I might have expected a few residential lots with some thirty-year-old houses. I would have even settled for a small variety store . . . but a landfill? To be fair, I have to add that most recently the same area has been redesigned as a beautiful new train station and commuter facility.

This was a symbolic omen of what happened to sports, at least for me. If I had stayed away, if I had not made that trip, I could have remembered the field the way it was that day in 1962.

5. No timeouts in life. No instant replays.

Most sporting events are bound in some way by a time element. In basketball, football, soccer, and hockey, the finality of the contest is managed by the clock. You play until time runs out. The advantage is that in all these sports you have an idea of how long that time is. Fifteen-minute quarters, twenty-minute halves, five-minute overtimes. In baseball, you have nine innings. Each team has nine chances to score or prevent the other team from scoring. Each inning is limited by three outs, and then you switch. Unless the game goes into extra innings, the end can be calculated. In all of these sports, if things are getting out of hand, you can call timeout. You can halt the progress and, in some cases, the momentum of the game by calling timeout.

Life isn't like sports. You can cease activity but you can't stop the clock. There are no timeouts. There are no do-overs, no Mulligans. You have to live with the results of what you have done, good or bad.

We live in a throwaway society. We want information faster and we want more choices. With all these choices, we still, at times, don't know what we want, and if we don't like what we have picked, we are ready to dump it and try again. This could be a burger, a car, or even a relationship. Imagine going into a new marriage and a lifetime relationship based on a prenuptial agreement, dividing the spoils of war in case the relationship goes sour. It's almost as if we are walking to the batter's box in a tight game, knowing full well that we are going to strike out, even before we face the first pitch.

The ironic part of life is that, at the end of the day, it is only a series of twenty-four-hour periods. If we can decide, as individuals, what the most important values are in our own personal lives, and then use those as guiding principles in what we do daily, we will be more likely to wade through much of the superficial garbage that life brings. We'll have a chance to concentrate on and develop what is most meaningful.

Finally, knowing what we know about how uncertain life is, we can learn to live each day as though it was our last day on earth, because someday it will be.

6. Pay it forward.

The expression "pay it forward" is used to describe the concept of asking the beneficiary of a good deed to repay it to others instead of the original benefactor.

I have always wanted to bury the bad and share the good. If there was a last piece of pie, I could never bring myself to eat it. It has never been enough for me to have a great experience. A great experience always becomes better when I have shared it with my wife, my family, a friend, or even a stranger. It could be a good joke, a good movie, the last piece of cake, or knowing what it's like to stand in that batter's box, staring down the pitcher on a warm summer day. Paying it forward is not as easy as it sounds. It's not something that you can put into your regular schedule, like taking your vitamins. It requires you to understand what your values and priorities are and to be observant enough to recognize the right opportunity and the right people to share with. Whatever you enjoy, whatever your gift, look for an opportunity to share it. Pay it forward.

7. You've gotta wanna.

You probably do the best job, learn the most, and are most committed to things you care about and are passionate about and would go to the wall for. At some point, you need to decide for yourself what those things are and then devote your time, passion, and skills to them. Never in life have I seen better examples of this than with parents and children. I have said many times throughout this book that I was, at least in my mind, born to be a dad. I was fortunate enough to be heavily involved in all three of my sons' trips through childhood, into adolescence, and eventually to manhood. While most parents were looking forward to their children moving out so that they could convert that last bedroom to a wet bar, pool table, and Jacuzzi, I would be happy to rewind the tape from eighteen back to eight and do it all over again. Life and relationships are too important to go through the motions.

8. Raising the bar.

Whether we are talking about sports or life, your children or someone else's, your spouse or yourself, if you expect good things, you will usually get them. Early in the book, I shared the story of our seven-year-olds executing the cutoff play when a ball was hit to the outfielders. The only limit keeping those kids from executing that skill apparently came from the league director, who felt they weren't old enough to grasp the concept. I didn't think they were too young, and they actually ended up doing a good job of relays in a game. If you gently nudge people to higher expectations, seasoned delicately with confidence and support, without being punitive, demanding, or cruel, it is amazing the results you can achieve.

9. Tomorrow is a new day and another game.

We all have our lists of victories and defeats, hardships and windfalls. Some of us have way more of one than the other, and I struggle at times on why that is. Some things that life throws at us are totally out of our control, and we have to play the hands we are dealt. Often, we go through years of conflict, turmoil, and grief largely as a result of our own doing. We all make good and bad decisions, and most times we live or die by the consequences of those decisions. The good news is in the old saying, "Every day is the first day of the rest of your life."

It's hard to endure a tough loss, wipe the slate clean, and play tomorrow's game with confidence. It's tough to draw a line in the sand, start over, have a new outlook on life, and mend a broken relationship. It's hard . . . but it can be done.

10. You're better than you think you are. It's mostly in your head.

I can't count the number of times, in and out of sports, where I have seen the benefits of having confidence, of believing in yourself. I have also seen the opposite, the negative effect of not having that self-assurance. From my early days as a Little Leaguer to my coaching days and eventually as a husband and father, I have learned that confidence can be your greatest ally; lacking it can be a huge weight hanging around your neck. For me, it was the day in the high school gym, yearbook in hand, when I vowed I would never be unprepared again.

I saw it later when coaching, seeing young Paul dragging his bat to the plate, bases loaded and two outs. He seemed to know that he was going to strike out. By the time he got into the batter's box, he had two strikes against him—in his own mind. When he finally did strike out to end the game, we tried not to even look at him as he returned with tears in his eyes.

They say a coward dies a thousand deaths but a hero only dies once. I think there is some truth and applicability to that here. Paul could have gone to the plate picturing himself getting the game-winning hit and being surrounded by jubilant teammates. He still might have struck out, ending the game, but he would have given his all and could have been confident in knowing there was nothing more he could do.

CHAPTER 8

Once a Fan, Always a Fan

Writing this book was, at times, like breaking open an old chest of memories and having them burst forth with details that I thought I had long since forgotten. In some respects, it brought a conscious perspective on how I used childhood experiences and memories to shape the man I was hoping to be. Certainly a large portion of it has been the rantings of a critical middle-aged weekend warrior that sees more and more of his sports life going on the shelf every year. I'll admit to being critical and ranting but offer an explanation that my wife used to give my boys: "I wouldn't yell at you if I didn't love you so much."

I have spent a lifetime watching, playing, coaching, and generally loving sports. I loved what it was and am disappointed in what it has become. I also know that we could resurrect much of what was good about sports. We could dust it off and give it to our children, who will be the adults and leaders of tomorrow. It's not too late.

There are as many hobbies as there are people. Everyone has their own interests, passions, and priorities. Not everyone is interested in sports. However, we all need a passion, a drive that sustains us along life's path. I am not suggesting that sports or any other form of recreation should be a substitute for your personal religious beliefs and values, but they are manmade institutions, which have throughout the years become a trademark of what is right and good in our lives. There is nothing that summarizes what sports was for me, what it has become, and what it could be again more than the following quote.

In the movie *Field of Dreams*, Terrance Mann (James Earl Jones) speaks prophetically and beautifully about the role baseball, indeed all sports, has played in the fabric of American culture. His famous soliloquy to Ray Kinsella (Kevin Costner) is a testament to the tradition and legacy of sports passed down from generation to generation.

Terence Mann: "Ray, people will come, Ray. The one constant through all the years, Ray, has been baseball. America has rolled by like an army of steamrollers. It has been erased like a blackboard, rebuilt, and erased again. But baseball has marked the time. This field, this game: it's a part of our past, Ray. It reminds us of all that once was good, and that could be again. Oh, people will come, Ray. People will most definitely come."

As a weather-beaten, experienced, sometimes frustrated senior citizen, I sit on an old stone wall out in the middle of a large field. Over my shoulder, I look back on the memories, the victories, the disappointments, and the bonding of former players, friends, coaches, and children reflected in these pages. I remember with sweet sadness teams that never changed and friends that were bonded together through participation as a team. I remember my idols in many professional sports that would have played the game for no pay.

As I look out in front of me, I see another large stretch of open field. I see the potential of what is yet to be, the future of sports, the potential for the honesty and beauty of pure competition. I see all the young children yet to play the game, a game, any game now that doesn't exclude girls and women from sharing the same rush that competition in sports can bring. My hope is that we find a way to return to the values of yesterday, values that spend less time treating sports and their teams and players as a greed-infested business and try to salvage some of what has made sport that immovable rock that Terrance Mann spoke of.

I hope this journey I've shared with you was entertaining. More importantly, I hope it provided an opportunity to pause and renew the values and experiences we have all had in our lives. Whether we are professional or amateur athletes, weekend warriors or just armchair fans, let us look for opportunities to weed out the bad and share the good. My hope is that before I get called home to that higher league in the sky, I can honestly say that I progressed from "Once a Fan, but No Longer" to "Once a Fan, Always a Fan."

My wife and I have made a conscious effort to look for daily opportunities to instill confidence and self-worth in our boys, without egotism. There will be times in life when that may be all you have. It is up to all of us to use the best of our memories and experiences to improve the quality and purpose of our own lives. It is also our challenge to use these experiences to reach out to others, to pay it forward, and to help guide and develop. Let's start today.

BIBLIOGRAPHY

Baseball Almanac. "The 1960 World Series." Accessed February 2012. http://www.baseball-almanac.com/ws/yr1960ws.shtml.

Deford, Frank. "Everything on the Line." *Sports Illustrated*. Posted July 17, 2007.
http://sportsillustrated.cnn.com/2007/writers/best_game/06/12/deford.best/.

Encyclopedia of World Biography. "Mickey Mantle Biography." Accessed April 2012.
http://www.notablebiographies.com/Lo-Ma/Mantle-Mickey.html.

Major League Baseball. "The 1975 World Series." Accessed January 2012. http://mlb.mlb.com/mlb/history/postseason/mlb_ws_recaps.jsp?feature=1975.

US Hockey Hall of Fame. "The 1980 US Olympic Team." Accessed April 2012.
http://www.usahockey.com/ushhof/default.aspx?NAV=AF_01&id=289718&DetailedNews=yes.